CANADIAN
BY CHOICE

CANADIAN BY CHOICE

Trudy Duivenvoorden Mitic

LANCELOT PRESS
HANTSPORT, NOVA SCOTIA

ISBN 0-88999-368-8
Cover design by Robert Pope
Second printing December 1988
Third printing February 1990

LANCELOT PRESS LIMITED
Hantsport, Nova Scotia
Office and production facilities on Hwy. No. 1, $\frac{1}{2}$ mile east of Hantsport.

TO CAROLINE AND AARON
the next generation

TO WAYNE
their father and my dearest friend

Contents

Prologue

This is the story of a young immigrant couple from the Netherlands and of the struggle through their early years in Canada. Filled with the vision of a better future in the New World, they arrived on Canadian soil in 1952, armed only with their hopes and dreams and with a dogged determination to succeed in the country of their choosing. They were quickly and unexpectedly relegated by the Canadian Government to a small isolated community in northern New Brunswick where they learned to cope with loneliness, near poverty, and the harsh winter climate typical of that region. As aliens in the tiny village of Jacquet River, they had to adjust to a new language and to a culture very different from the one that they had been so accustomed to.

Holland in the early 1950s was a country struggling to recover from the devastation of five long years of German oppression. Stripped entirely of her resources and with her cities reduced to a mass of diseased and poverty-stricken people, she could offer little hope to the youth of that day who had spent the previous half decade hiding and waiting.

Gerard Duivenvoorden and Sjaan van Schie had grown up on farms in the neighbouring rural communities of Rijpwetering and Oud Ade in western Holland. Long before the end of the German occupation, they had decided that one day, when stability had been returned to their country, they would marry and purchase a dairy farm of their own.

During the Occupation, their farming families had been among the lucky few; although money was scarce, there had never been any fear of starving to death. A testimony to this was the frequent queue of city folk on their doorsteps, begging for the chance to work in return for a square meal. Gerard's mother remembers that it was not uncommon to have prominent professionals from Amsterdam scrubbing her kitchen floor as payment for a simple meal of potatoes and vegetables.

Powerless and penniless but with their precious health intact, the families of Gerard and Sjaan had emerged after the liberation of their country to find a once proud and independent nation smouldering in total and utter ruination. Everywhere the swollen landscape had been littered with the souls of the homeless, the destitute, the hopeless.

After the Occupation, Gerard had sailed to Indonesia where he spent three years in the service of the Dutch armed forces as part of a peacekeeping corps. He had returned home with three years of wages in his pocket and with the intention of finally being able to marry his long time bride-to-be.

Together the young couple had eagerly sought to purchase a farm but were soon made aware of the futility of their search. Holland in the early 1950s had a surplus of fifty thousand young farmers and a serious scarcity of land for agricultural use.

Canada in the 1950s, on the other hand, was in dire need of capable farmers to work the miles and miles of land that had lain idle for too long. Canada too had felt the effects of the war: she had weathered a severe depression and a food shortage while her many natural resources had lain unused and undeveloped. The Canadian Government had been eager to ensure that this situation would never again be duplicated; consequently it had issued an invitation to foreign farmers to come to Canada and make it their home.

The resulting post-war of immigration that swept hundreds of thousands of newcomers to Canada had ensured that this country would never be the same again. Even as history was being made, Canada's social make-up was being irrevocably changed as one ocean liner after another, filled to repletion with immigrant hopefuls, had steamed its way across the Atlantic Ocean to the Port of Halifax.

Swept into this infectious tide was Gerard and Sjaan, at first hesitantly and then more eagerly. From newspapers and travel workshops they hungrily gleaned any and all information about Canada. Hastily they completed a short course on the English language that was to leave them ill-equipped to cope on Canadian soil, they later were to realize.

The Dutch Government too, had supported the emigration of a large number of its people to Canada. A restriction to this movement however, was that only people and not their money would be allowed to leave the country. Emigrants could take with them only a maximum of one hundred dollars per person. For Gerard and Sjaan, this had meant leaving behind a sizable nest egg and once again being plunged into poverty.

Holding firm to their decision to go to Canada nevertheless, they had been married in Oud Ade on June 17, 1952 and had started their journey across the Atlantic one day later.

The young couple that you will meet in the following pages are my parents. They were both twenty-six years of age when they arrived in Canada, he a tall, undaunted youth with a finely chiseled face and intense eyes of deep blue. Any hat that adorned his head was proudly tilted at a forty-five degree angle and worn like a personal trademark. She, the eldest daughter in a family of fifteen children, was a likeable young woman with a shy smile and a quick blush. Her quiet, unassuming way and her slight, physical stature served well to camouflage a strength of character that could not be undermined.

The story which has been re-created here is factual, accurate in detail, and entirely their own. The good life that they sought and eventually found here is testimony to the reason why so many thousands of immigrants have chosen Canada as their new home. As well and perhaps even more so, it is testimony to the resilience of my parents, their wonderful resourcefulness, and their unswerving optimism and determination.

1.

The Storm Lantern

I must not cry for it will do not an ounce of good. Thousands of miles away from my beloved parents and dear brothers and sisters, I sit in a dark, lonely room in an alien land. My bridegroom lies in the bed beside me, sleeping the dreamless slumber of the exhausted.

So much has happened since our wedding in Holland, just ten days ago. "Such spirited adventurers we are," we had thought smugly to ourselves as we had booked our passage to Canada, "to be married one day and depart for Canada the next." Our wedding had been a joyous occasion, with friends and neighbours alike wishing us well and marvelling at our courage and sense of adventure.

At the Port of Rotterdam, we had clung to our parents and siblings in an attempt to preserve these last few precious moments and commend them to our memory. Knowing that these memories are all we would have in Canada, we had tenaciously embraced our loved ones, all the while exchanging trembling whispers and misty smiles.

"Are you sure you have everything now? Did you remember that pair of wool slacks? After all, they say that it's cold in Canada."

"And you speak so little English. How will you cope?"

11

"Don't worry. We'll be okay. And we do have each other."

"Send us your address as soon as you know."

"Please write soon."

"We'll pray for you."

"Please don't cry."

The passage across the Atlantic proved to be a seven-day ordeal, especially for me. Our troubles began shortly after boarding the *Groote Beer*, a large and majestic ocean liner. No sooner were we out of the harbour when we were summoned to the officer's station and informed that the berth which we had so carefully reserved weeks before would not be available, due to overbooking. Despite our protestations we were tersely ushered to our separate quarters, Gerard to a berth he was to share with a half dozen other men, and I to a dormitory containing at least forty women and children.

With my head reeling from the shock of this new and unexpected development, I proceeded to stash my few pieces of baggage under the narrow bunk. Having done this, I sank wearily onto the bed and drew the little curtain, creating a dark and gloomy corner that was to be my only real haven of privacy throughout the voyage. There I collected my thoughts and willed away the feelings of depression that were already beginning to gnaw at the edges of my mind.

Once my composure had been solidly regained, I hurried back up to the deck to find an equally unhappy Gerard waiting for me. There we huddled together and discussed a new fear which had only just begun to creep into our minds — the fear of losing control over our own destiny.

Before my first day at sea was over, I began to experience the telltale symptoms of seasickness, an ailment that would stay with me for the duration of the voyage. At first I did my best to ignore the queasiness in the pit of my stomach. I continued to eat heartily, almost as if to defy the nasty beast. However, I soon was forced to give in to frequent bouts of vomiting that left me weak and lethargic.

Finally, too weak and emaciated to muster up even the desire to move, I confined myself to my little bunk, far away from sunshine and fresh air. I had never been this ill before.

12

Even here, deep within the bowels of the boat, the incessant rocking continued to play havoc with my stomach.

With Gerard sitting anxiously at my side we held vigil over our hopes and dreams. At that point, all we were were just two immigrant hopefuls together in that dark dank hole. I am most grateful that our parents did not see us in that state.

I was not the only passenger to succumb to seasickness. As the days went by, more and more people fell victim to severe nausea. Large barrels were set up in the dormitories as a substitute for "seasick bags." Sometimes we made it to the barrels on time, often we didn't. The barrels also became convenient receptacles for other items associated with daily living, including used diapers. The ensuing stench of sour vomit and dirty diapers was enough to send even the strongest stomachs into severe spasms of queasiness. Many of those who had up until this point successfully staved off seasickness, now found themselves hanging over the barrels and retching uncontrollably.

The crew tried in vain to keep the washrooms and dormitories reasonably clean. The salt water that they used to mop up the floors only added to the miry texture of what was already underfoot. The barrels were dutifully emptied overboard and presented for our use once again.

All around me the weak cries of sick children and the retching and moaning continued through the days and the nights. Looking back, I am amazed that with 747 passengers on board, the majority of whom were desperately ill, no one had actually died during the voyage. We Dutch must be a resilient lot!

Finally, mercifully, the *Groote Beer* sidled into her berth at Halifax. For the passengers, setting foot on solid ground was something that we had dreamed and talked about for days. I struggled up from my bunk for the last time as we hastily collected first my belongings and then Gerard's, and proceeded to join the crowds on deck. There, a festive atmosphere prevailed with the passengers straining over the railings, laughing, cheering, shaking hands, and clapping each other on the shoulder.

Even the dreary Halifax waterfront could do nothing to quell the enthusiasm of the group. Like prisoners waiting to be set free, we milled about the Canadian Immigration officials who had boarded, anxiously waiting to be called forward. Finally, after what seemed like an endless wait, we were beckoned by an official who consulted his clipboard momentarily and then nodded in our direction.

"Mr. and Mrs. Duivenvoorden?"

"Yes," be both hastened to reply.

"Ah, yes. . . you will be travelling by train to Dalhousie Junction in the province of New Brunswick, where arrangements have been made for you to work on a farm owned by a Mr. Black, your appointed sponsor."

"Where is New Brunswick?", we asked.

"Near Nova Scotia."

"And where is Nova Scotia?"

"You are in Nova Scotia."

"Oh."

"Why not," we said to each other as we proceeded down the ship's ramp. "One strange place is as good as another."

In that instant I could not help but glance one last time at the Dutch flag flying high above our heads on the ship's mast. We were about to sever our final link with our Homeland, our past, and all that was dear and familiar to us. With one more decisive step, we were off the ramp and on Canadian land. We had arrived at last!

On the waterfront, we were given some time to examine our new and unfamiliar surroundings. As we strolled along the dock, our first impression was one of vast open spaces and few people to fill them. On board the ship, our group of passengers had seemed immense, filling the vessel to repletion. Now, on the vast harbourfront, we amounted to but a few dots of people here and there.

As Gerard and I walked, we shared our impressions in hushed tones, almost as if we were afraid of being overheard even though there was no one else around. It seemed as if no one lived here; the entire waterfront looked sleepy and uninhabited. We were awestruck by the new sense of freedom that was beginning to prevail over us. In Rotterdam the congestion had been almost unbearable and our movement had been restricted to designated holding areas. Here we were seemingly allowed to roam freely, to linger where we wished.

The dock and surrounding walkways and warehouses were a drab, dirty grey, as if intentionally outfitted in grimy work clothes. Near the pier was an old fish shed with the remnants of many fish strewn carelessly about. Overhead, a raucous group of seagulls dipped and soared repeatedly over this feeding area. As we paused to watch their antics, the putrid smell of rotten fish reached our unsuspecting nostrils. Recoiling from the intensity of the stench, we quickly turned and hastened in the other direction.

Well away from the fish shed, we slowed our pace and resumed our leisurely stroll, enjoying the warmth of the summer sun. In the distance we saw who we assumed to be our first real Canadian, a young man sauntering along the dock. As we walked, he jingled some coins in the pockets of his trousers. We have never seen this practise before so surely this must be the Canadian way to display one's personal wealth. He was a very ordinary looking chap, though. Perhaps all Canadians are financially comfortable!

After a half-hour stroll along the waterfront, we were summoned to Pier 21, a large facility operated by the Immigration people. There we were gathered in a large assembly hall to again wait our turn, this time to be processed as landed immigrants. All around us people milled in small whirlpools, attempting to keep children, luggage, and documents together. The chattering was loud and incessant and the queasiness, which had just begun to lie dormant within me, was threatening to present itself once again. Finally we were summoned to appear before the officials. Nervously, we produced our papers and stood ready to answer questions with the help of a translator.

The procedure was quickly completed and our documents were stamped. We were then briskly waved in the direction of a nearby train station where the immigrant train stood waiting for our group's embarkment.

The squalid conditions that greeted us on board the train shocked us momentarily. The cars were gloomy and musty, with bare dirty floors and small wooden straight-backed seats. The bathrooms were cramped and smelled vaguely of chemical cleansers and of urine.

Still, a boisterous mood prevailed, as passengers jostled

each other in an attempt to find seats and luggage space. People were chatting noisily, addressing conductors in a unique blend of Dutch and broken English, and loudly summoning their children to selected seats.

"Hey, what do you think of this train?"

"Reminds me of what they used to cart people off to concentration camps!"

"Perhaps that is where we are going."

"Heaven only knows where we are going!"

It was mid-afternoon before the train pulled sluggishly away from the Halifax station. As I settled into my seat I suddenly realized that, for the first time in a week, I was hungry. Since the train had no dining nor canteen facilities, I had to settle for a chocolate bar which Gerard had purchased at the station.

From our vantage point near the grimy window, we noted the miles and miles of undisturbed forests, broken only by the occasional small farm or sleepy village. Here and there hilly meadows were dotted with a cow or two and perhaps a horse with his head hung low over the fence, totally oblivious to the roar of the passing train.

As the day wore on, conversation waned and weary passengers began to nod and sway to the rhythm of the rails. The constant clackety-clack of steel on steel became the prevailing sound as both children and adults grew quieter. Sleep was elusive however, the cramped space and ungiving seats had seen to that. We squirmed restlessly, trying in vain to settle into positions that would be bearably comfortable.

The hours ticked by slowly as the train continued into the night. Exhausted and hungry, we waited to see where we would be deposited, where we would start our new life. I huddled closer to Gerard, not at all sure that I was ready to face this final unknown.

At 11:00 p.m. we were startled out of our drowsy state by a sudden, loud call which rang through our car: DAL-H-O-U-SIE JUNCTION-N-N! This was the train's first stop, and our destination. Quickly we scrambled into our coats and collected our baggage as the train came to an abrupt stop, its wheels squealing in loud protest. Without fanfare we were briskly ushered onto the windy platform. A moment later the train was again on its way, its heaviness resonating against the night sky.

There we stood in the darkness, just the two of us, uncertain what to do next. In the distance a lone figure was slowly approaching, a storm lantern swaying periously at his side. As he neared he raised the lantern high above his head and beckoned us to follow him to a small, desolate stone building that stood nearby.

Once inside, the stationmaster placed the smoky lantern on the counter top and began to study the papers that we had proffered. As he hunched over the documents in the sallow light, the lantern flame alternately flickered and flared, sending eerie shadows dancing on the bare, unpainted walls. Ever so carefully, my husband and I dared to exchange an anxious glance.

Oh Lord, was this to be our destination? This God-forsaken place that seemed to lament of loneliness and isolation, isolation so complete that it did not even have electricity? What sort of backwoods place had we been sentenced to?

As desperate thoughts raced through my mind, I heard the stationmaster's distant voice, kindly and in an attempt to be reassuring, "We're having a power outage. Nothing to get concerned about. The lights should be back on soon. I'll call Mr. Black, who lives in Eel River just a few miles away, to come to get you."

Fifteen minutes later we were huddled together in the ramshackle cab of an old pick-up truck, finally on our way to our new home. As we pulled up to the farm house, I noticed with relief the bright light pouring from a number of the long narrow windows. Thank heaven the electricity had been restored!

Once inside, we were greeted not unkindly but with some degree of reservation and restraint. "Hello, we've been expecting you. Your names are . . . Gerard and who? Shawne? Must be Jane in English. Come, you must be very tired. Let us show you to your room. Goodnight!"

So ends our very first day in Canada. I must attempt to empty my mind of the loneliness that has already settled there and to get some sleep, even though I know my efforts will be in

17

vain. Already I see a band of pale light beginning to form in the eastern sky. The rising sun will unveil a whole new world to us, a world for which I am not at all ready. Can it be possible that we will ever really belong here?

2.

Twenty Dollars a Week

Our new world is still so uncertain; our old world seems years away. We are trying so hard to make this way of life ours, but things are not well. The frown lines on Gerard's forehead seem to furrow deeper every day, and now he speaks of running away. But where would we run to? We do not know a soul in this small rural area and have no idea what lies beyond its boundaries.

The morning after we arrived, we awoke to brilliant sunshine streaming in through our bedroom window. We dressed quickly, speaking all the while in hushed whispers. What, in our woefully inadequate English, would we say to our employer? Hopefully our eager smiles and firm handshakes would convey our intention to please. After more than a week of travel, we were eager to assume some sort of daily routine.

Hesitantly, we started down the stairs, hand in hand. In the kitchen the family was waiting to greet us. A deeply wrinkled elderly woman of generous proportion, two stout and robust middle-aged men and a younger, frail looking woman sat around a large table in the centre of the room. In a corner, away from the group, sat a small, fragile old man who spoke nary a word.

The pale green kitchen contained a large cast iron stove

whose overbearing black pipe dominated the decor as it rose to meet the plaster ceiling high above our heads. The small wooden counter set against one wall contained a varied collection of dirty breakfast dishes. Next to the counter was a small enamelled basin and a drainboard. Directly above this hung a tattered grouping of tea and hand towels.

The large table was bare except for two small clean plates, presumably placed there for our breakfast. We were beckoned to sit, and heaping bowls of steaming porridge were placed in front of us. As we ate in silence, the family members were introduced, each eyeing us in turn with some consternation. Certainly they must have wondered about my ability to put in a full day of hard work; after a week of nausea and abstention from food, I could not have been a picture of glowing health!

After breakfast, one of the middle-aged men motioned to Gerard to follow him outside. My spouse and I exchanged an encouraging smile and then he stepped through a doorway, the screen door slamming in his wake. I was on my own! I breathed deeply, smoothed my cotton apron, and awaited further direction.

"Come with me," the old woman beckoned with the crook of her finger. I followed her down a set of steep narrow stairs into a dank smelling, dimly lit basement. She motioned to an enormous pile of soiled clothing, a washbasin, a few buckets, and a box of soap powder. After speaking a few curt words which I failed to comprehend, she labored slowly up the stairs, heaving from the effort, and finally disappeared through the trapdoor in the ceiling.

If it was laundry they wanted me to do, fine, I would do it, every stitch of it! I would scrub the whites until they shone. I would wrestle with the heavy work clothes until they were cleaner than they had been in some time. My arms ached to get started as I filled the basin with hot, soapy water. Oh, this felt so good! I wondered how Gerard was doing and what he would have to tell me at coffee break. In Holland, the entire country breaks for a mid-morning "bakje" and it is a most enjoyable time.

"No, I must not think of Holland," I chided myself as I rinsed a basin full of laundry, wringing each item vigorously in turn. With a bucket of heavy, wet clothing in each hand, I stepped carefully up to the kitchen and out through the screen door. Oh, heavenly outdoors! The sun felt delicious on my face as I pinned work pants and pillowcases alike to the tottering line. I took in my surroundings as I emptied first one bucket and then the other.

The landscape here is so different, not at all like the endlessly flat terrain that I am accustomed to. There are trees in every direction and rail fences that run up and down the pastures like stitches on a giant patchwork. The green landscape is dotted with many rocks and boulders, each in its own nest of undisturbed long grass. The yard is overgrown with wildflowers that are splendid in color and fragrance. And the sky! It is magnificent and more blue than anything I have ever seen before!

Where was Gerard? I squinted in the direction of the old weather-beaten barn but saw no sign of him. I picked up the buckets and returned to the basement, ready to do battle with yet another pile of dirty clothing.

The call to come to lunch was a most welcome one. I was so happy to see my Gerard once again! He had spent most of the morning in the fields and was grateful to be momentarily out of the sun. Our meal was eaten largely in silence, we two at one end of the table, and our hosts spread around the other three sides.

I spent the afternoon in the sewing room, where I enthusiastically tackled a formidable stack of items waiting to be mended. Supper was eaten in much the same atmosphere as lunch. The food was plain but good, although we admittedly could have eaten more, had it been offered.

When all the evening chores were finally completed, Gerard and I treated ourselves to a leisurely stroll. Arm in arm we walked, reiterating our dreams and plans. "This is only for a year," Gerard kept saying, "then we'll be on our own. We can handle it."

As the last traces of sunlight waned in the western sky, we returned gingerly to the house. The family was gathered in the sitting room. Not sure whether we should join them uninvited, we waited for a moment in the narrow, shadowy hallway. Finally we ventured in timidly to bid them good-night, and then we climbed up the stairs to our bedroom.

Our first two weeks have been spent much the same as that first day. On the second day, our precious "kist" arrived, containing all of our belongings. Like children at Christmas, we opened the large wooden container and lovingly transferred its contents to our bedroom. As we worked, the sights and even the smells of our beloved homeland enveloped us. As I fingered the crisp linens and caressed the delicate china, I tried to dwell on the future and not think about the past. Someday my own home will be adorned with these dear and familiar items and perhaps then I may feel that I truly belong here.

Also on our second day, we dared to ask if we could make a cup of coffee, using our own instant coffee and sugar that some thinking relative had suggested we bring with us. The old lady, obviously the matriarch of the family, nodded her consent but pointed to the wood stove and proceeded to put the electric hot plate away. Obviously it was not meant for our use. We were somewhat taken aback by this unfriendly act but nevertheless fired up the old stove and sat waiting for the water to boil.

At the end of the week, we eagerly anticipated that we would soon be paid for our first week's work. The subject of wages had not been discussed but we reasoned that if we worked hard, then surely they would be pleased with us and pay us fairly.

When we were finally summoned to the kitchen, the old lady sat waiting for us, clasping a fist full of tattered bills. Very carefully she counted out twenty dollars and placed all but a one-dollar bill on the table in front of Gerard. "What about me?", I thought. "Haven't I done your laundry, mended your clothing, baked your bread, and scrubbed your floors?"

"What about Sjaan?", Gerard asked cautiously.

"That is for both of you," she responded sternly and with finality. "The government says that we don't have to pay you any more than twenty dollars a week. If you don't like it, you don't have to stay."

As we sat numbed, she continued, "I am keeping one

dollar back as your payment for the milk that you have used in your coffee."

Speechless, we rose from the table and made our way up to our room, where Gerard vented his frustrations in loud angry whispers. Our long hard days of labor had produced but a mere nineteen dollars. At this rate, we would never be able to have our own farm. Tired, dejected, and lonely, we held each other tightly in an attempt to be consoled.

On Sunday, our situation continued to worsen. After breakfast we inquired about church and asked if we might be given a ride, since the family was obviously preparing to attend as well.

"Which church?", the old lady asked.

"A Catholic Church, if possible."

"Hah!", she snorted. "In that case you can walk. It's only a few miles up the road."

As we started out in the direction she had indicated, she called after us, "If you change your mind about your church you can ride with us. If not, walk!"

Our second week here has been almost unbearable. We are no longer permitted to speak Dutch at mealtime. Indeed, the meals themselves have become an ordeal. Although the food is good and nourishing, the rations have become increasingly meagre. If we dare to ask for another slice of bread, the old lady marches wordlessly to the pantry, and returns with a single slice of bread which she drops on the place of the person who requested it, usually Gerard. Sometimes Gerard will ask for me as well. Again she will rise without expression and fetch another single slice from the pantry which she then drops on my plate.

I worry about Gerard. I know he is working hard and not eating as well as he should be. Thank God we are young and healthy, but where will it all end?

It has been a long rainy evening and we have been confined to our own room as usual. Gerard lies on the bed and stares at the naked walls, all the while worrying about our predicament. I always end my day with a fervent prayer that things might soon be better for us. In the meantime, we hope and we continue to do the best we can here.

3.

A Daring Venture

Instead of fretting helplessly, I should this very moment be praying fervently for Gerard's safe return! Early this morning he struck out on foot for the village of Jacquet River in search of the priest whom we met at church last Sunday. We have no idea where Jacquet River is, but Gerard was adamant that he would find it. Now it is mid-afternoon and I am worried sick that I might never see him again. Then what would become of me, a poor immigrant woman who really has no idea where she is, and not nearly enough money to return home!

Oh God, I must not think about that; I must not allow myself to be worried into a state of frenzy! Surely Gerard will return soon with good news and then we can pack up our belongings and leave this dreaded place forever.

This past week has been hell for both of us. We are no longer allowed to eat our meals together for we "talk too much." I now have my meals brought to me in the sewing room where I spend much of my time mending and ironing. My darling and I do not see each other from six o'clock in the morning until eight o'clock in the evening or later, when all of the day's chores have finally been completed.

This increased isolation has only served to intensify my loneliness. Sometime, within the confines of this unadorned little room, I imagine myself to be sitting at my mother's sewing machine in Holland, my sisters mere footsteps away, their noisy chatter and laughter rising up from various parts of the house to greet me. I strain my ears and listen, but hear only the incessant droning of the bulbous, neon-tipped houseflies that hover perpetually around the edges of the uncurtained window panes.

Gerard has been doing most of the farm work by himself while the men "go to town" and find other reasons to be away. Gerard doesn't mind though; at least he can work in peace and do things his own way.

We do not mind the hard work; it is the unfriendliness and overt discrimination that we were not at all prepared for. We feel so unwelcome here . . . and yet, these are the very people who have entered into an agreement with the Government to open their home to foreign workers, to orient us to the Canadian way of life, and to help us on our way to independence. Surely not all Canadians are this unfeeling and uncaring!

It seems that we no longer have any privacy, even in the night. A few nights ago we were abruptly awakened when our bedroom door, which has no lock, was suddenly opened. In the doorway stood one of the two younger men, the stout, thick-necked one who is married to the frail, sad-faced young girl who never speaks. With a wicked and lascivious smile on his face, he strode over to our bed and perched himself solidly at my feet.

"How's everything going?", he asked, winking in my direction. I cringed under the covers as Gerard told him in no uncertain terms to leave our room immediately! Unhurriedly, he rose from the bed and strolled to the door.

"Let me know if you need me," he again winked in my direction and, laughing rudely, closed the door noisily behind him.

It seems that now, on top of everything else we have our safety to worry about as well! Oh, darling husband, please let me see you walking up the lane the next time I look out of the window! Without you, I don't know what would become of me here . . .

Yesterday, Sunday, we again walked to church, grateful to be away from the farm for even just an hour or two. The Latin service, with which we are so well acquainted, offers a brief but welcome respite from our own anxieties. Observing the visiting pastor as he solemnly performed all of the familiar rituals, I could not help but indulge in a desperate prayer to my God.

"Oh Dear Lord, please help us to see our way through this trial of ours. If only the pastor could speak our language, then we could explain our situation and seek his advice! What a luxury it would be to have someone with whom we could converse, someone we could trust. Lord, I have no business bothering You with my trivia, You who certainly must have more important matters to tend to. I thank You for our health and pray for added strength (which we will need!). Amen."

The service over, we made our way to the rear of the church, ready to stroll as slowly as possible back to the dreaded farm.

"Excuse me! Excuse me! Sir! Madam?", a clear, young voice called suddenly from behind us. We turned to see an altar server, a boy no more than ten years old, hastily approach us while at the same time struggling with his cumbersome ankle-length robe.

"Father would like to see you. Can you wait?"

Not fully comprehending, uncertain that we had heard correctly, we waited hesitantly for several minutes on the steps of the tiny church.

"Hello. Hoe maken jullie het? How are you?" a voice boomed suddenly through the small portal as the visiting pastor came forward to greet us, offering both hands which we clasped ever so tightly! Not daring to believe our sudden good fortune, I gazed drunkenly at this man as he proceeded to introduce himself in our language. Gerard was smiling from ear to ear, the first time in many days, and I . . . I could have hugged that man, that gift from God, except that the Church would have certainly frowned upon my brazen display of gratitude!

"I am Father Bergman, a native of Belgium and a member of the Salesian order," the priest was saying. "We operate Don Bosco College, a school for boys in Jacquet

27

River, several miles from here. On Sundays, we sometimes substitute for the parish priests who are ill or away."

"Which is why I am here today," he added as an afterthought, smiling warmly at us. "The altar boys told me that a young Dutch couple was among my congregation today. Tell me about yourselves. What brings you to this part of the world?"

Needing no further coaxing, we poured out our story. We spoke of our precious hopes and dreams for a better life in Canada. Like a tap under pressure that has finally been opened, we spilled out the sordid details of our current situation. Could he understand that, with no one to speak to, to turn to, we felt trapped like two desperate souls hopelessly tangled in a perpetual nightmare?

"This is not right," he finally said, shaking his head and frowning deeply. "You must not think that these people are typical of all Canadians. Canadians are a warm and generous people. As for your situation, it is not good and something must be done to help you. Perhaps," he added slowly, thoughtfully, "the Salesians might be able to come to your aid."

"Aside from the school, we also own a farm," he continued. "We purchased the property several years ago with the intent of using it to teach our youngsters to farm. In so doing, we had visions of establishing a thriving and profitable enterprise. Things have not worked out that way though, and the place has become somewhat dilapidated from lack of use. It seems that we priests were not cut out to nurture the harvests of this world!", he chuckled with a twinkle in his eye.

"For some time we have been discussing the possibility of installing a manager on the property, a farmer who could restore it to a profitable state. If we decide to do this, would you be interested in living there and managing the place for us?" At this point he turned slightly to look directly at us, assessing us keenly, waiting to witness our reaction.

Would we? WOULD we? We could hardly contain our joy, yet we dared not believe what we were hearing. Surely God had heard my desperate prayer, had decided to intervene for two pitiful and homeless beings! Well, we would rise to the challenge, work like two souls possessed, and restore that farm to something they could be proud of!

"Yes, Father, we would be very interested," we answered timidly, still not daring to hope that our fortunes were about to change.

"Good! I'll let my superiors know and we'll contact you in a few days. I know where you are staying. I must caution you though, that our farm is generally in poor shape and will require a lot of hard work. The house may shock you, it has not been lived in for several years and has seriously deteriorated. In its present state, it is hardly the place for a young family."

While he spoke, my mind raced along at a perilous rate. Please see fit to give us a chance, I silently implored. We won't disappoint you. That old house will be like a seat in heaven for us! You won't regret hiring us! Can't you see the desperation in our eyes?

"And now, I must get back to the school," Father's voice nudged me unwillingly back to the present. "Don't despair, and don't give up," he declared authoritatively, shaking our hands firmly as if to inject us with an added dose of spiritual strength. "Remember that God is with you."

Entranced, we walked back to the Black farm, periodically stopping to reassure each other that we had indeed heard what seemed too wonderful to be true. Even at the farm, our good spirits continued to prevail as we shared knowing smiles and delicious secrets.

"What are you so happy about?", the old woman demanded to know, her voice laced with suspicion. 'Surely she will not allow us to go to church next Sunday,' I thought to myself as I continued with my chores. 'That is, IF we are still here then,' I added silently, smiling inwardly.

Early this morning, Gerard bounded out of bed with renewed vigor and energy. "As soon as the morning chores are finished, I am walking to Jacquet River to speak with Father Bergman and his colleagues," he announced as he hurriedly donned his workclothes.

"What about me?", I asked cautiously. "You don't plan to leave me here with these people! You haven't even the faintest idea where you are going!"

"You, my dear, had best stay here and go about your daily chores, pretending all is normal today. I will tell them that I am going on some personal business. They will let me go." As he exuberantly waltzed me around the tiny bedroom, he continued, "My darling, soon we will be on our own, in our own home, and far away from here.

"And don't be afraid of that big oaf. He may leer at you but he would never dare touch you! I'll be back before you know it. Remember that I love you!"

I trudged through the Monday morning laundry ritual, trying not to worry about Gerard. During lunch with the family, I answered their pointed and persistent questions with a blank stare and a shrug of my shoulders. Banished to the sewing room, I mended with a fervor, trying to stave off a desperation that was beginning to grow inside of me. Where are you, Gerard? You should have been back by now!

On I continued, pushing the needle into the cloth and pulling the thread through, ad infinitum. When I painfully jabbed my weary fingers with a needle, my last steely ounce of composure was finally and completely crumbled. I fled to my room, slammed the door, and burst uncontrollably into tears.

Here I have sat for the last two hours, praying and waiting . . . waiting.

Oh Joyous Day, my darling returned late this afternoon with wonderful news! We are going to Jacquet River TONIGHT! I must quell the urge to dance euphorically around the room and concentrate instead on Gerard's words as he recounts the day's adventure.

After leaving me this morning, my hero walked briskly for about an hour before assuming that he must be in or near Jacquet River. After all, he reasoned, in Holland a fifteen or twenty minute stroll will see you from one village to the next. However, we are rapidly discovering that this is not the case in Canada!

To continue, Gerard had walked at length and was now trying to determine if he had arrived at his destination, or if he was anywhere near it, for that matter. With no signposts in sight to guide him, he walked to the nearest house and knocked on the door. The lady who answered gently informed him that he was still in Eel River and that Jacquet River was yet another twenty miles away!

"Shall I call a taxi for you?", she offered.

An hour later, Gerard arrived at the College where he was warmly greeted by Father Bergman who, thank Heaven, hadn't forgotten about us and had already spoken to the Superior. The final details of our employment were quickly mapped out and, after a hurried visit to the farm, an inwardly ecstatic Gerard stepped back into the taxi cab for the return trip to Eel River.

"I worried about you," he confessed upon his arrival as we embraced in the driveway. "Throughout the day I kept thinking, my God, I've left her there, all alone with those hostile strangers. You are okay, aren't you?", he asked anxiously, gently nuzzling my nose with his.

"Only worried," I smiled through my sticky, drying tears.

From around the corner of the house young Black suddenly appeared, bellowing at us, "You are late! Where the hell were you?" Striding forbodingly toward us with arm raised and one stubby finger pointed in the direction of the barn, he bawled to Gerard, "Start those chores immediately if you don't want to get kicked off this farm right now! Now get!"

"I'm staying with you," I said quickly to Gerard as I stepped up to him and decisively linked my arm with his.

"Good idea," he replied. "As soon as the chores are done, we'll tell them that we're leaving."

"When are the Fathers coming for us?"

"I'm not sure. It will probably be fairly late. Don't worry. They will come."

Young Black stood menacingly in the yard and glowered at us as we retreated hastily to the barn.

Two hours later, the chores completed, we nervously entered the kitchen where the family was congregated for supper. With the aroma of beef stew in our nostrils, we explained in our best English that we would be leaving their farm to accept other employment.

The explosion of anger was instant and spontaneous.

"What? Leaving? What a laugh! You are bluffing! You

31

have nowhere to go! Why, no one in his right mind will hire two dim-wits who don't even speak English!"

"We are going to work for the Salesian Fathers in Jacquet River."

"For those god-damned black crows? And exactly when do you propose to leave?"

"Tonight."

"Tonight? This evening? Well, get out of this house! Get out right now and don't come back!"

We made a very hasty exit and the door was slammed behind us with ungiving finality.

Hungry, weary, and somewhat bewildered, we stood in the yard for several long, silent moments, wondering what to do. The prospect of having to go back into that house to pack our precious belongings made me cower involuntarily.

"Come, my dear," Gerard said consolingly, taking my hand in his. "We will walk over to the neighbours and ask them for a bite to eat."

"But we can't! We've only met them once or twice!"

"Yes we can. Now come along."

The neighbours greeted us kindly, offered us sandwiches, and mercifully refrained from asking questions.

Back at the Black farm, we timidly entered the house, slunk quickly up the stairs, and took refuge in our little room. There we set about packing our things in makeshift boxes and containers.

It is now dark and we have been waiting restlessly for the last two hours. Gerard is endlessly pacing the floor and peering out of the window into the blackness. It will be most consoling to finally see the approaching headlights of those who will deliver us from this purgatory.

"Here they come!", Gerard has just announced jubilantly from the window.

And so, suddenly, it is over. Goodbye, Room! Goodbye, House! Goodbye, People! We are on our way!

4.

Under Our Own Roof

I am feeling positively jubilant this evening, sitting at a huge old wooden table in a cavernous kitchen. I AM IN MY OWN HOME! We arrived late yesterday evening, having been transported here by a jovial young Salesian religious, a Brother Gerard.

Not a word was said at the Black home as we hastily transferred our belongings from our room to the waiting truck in the yard. No handshakes, no sentiments of remorse were offered. A full week's wages was owed to us but this was not given and we dared not ask for it.

Timidly we called out our goodbyes as we climbed into the cab of the truck. Then, without fanfare, we rolled out of the driveway and started on our journey to sweet and delicious freedom!

Behind the wheel of the dusty old panel truck, Brother kept up a steady "conversation" with us, sprinkling his words liberally with vigorous nods and cheerful chuckles. His splendid baritone, even though it insisted on speaking in a foreign tongue, was most consoling! For the first time in six weeks I could feel myself beginning to relax.

Upon our arrival at this house, Brother Gerard roused a sleeping youth who had presumably been stationed here to keep watch over the farm. The lad quickly dressed and packed his few belongings while Brother explained that someone from the College would arrive in the morning to give us a tour of the place. Bidding us goodnight, he departed into the darkness, with the sleepy-eyed youth reluctantly in tow. I assume the lad's sleep was interrupted to give us some privacy as well as the only bed in the house!

Hand in hand and barely able to contain our excitement, we walked from room to room, exploring our surroundings. We marvelled at the size of the house, with its nine bedrooms, bathroom, kitchen and sitting and dining rooms. As I was enthusiastically starting up my third set of stairs, Gerard stopped me with a gentle, teasing smile.

"You've been up those stairs already."

Politely but with a most amused expression on his face, he showed me the two staircases and explained how we had gone up one, come down the other, and thus had come full circle. Still smiling, he patted my arm as if to console me for my extremely poor sense of direction!

Before we finally climbed into the still warm bed, I tried to insist that we should at least change the sheets and pillowcases.

"You want to unpack NOW, at midnight?", asked my husband as he proceeded to make himself comfortable beneath the covers.

First thing this morning, I unpacked my linens and changed the bed!

It is heavenly to finally be on our own; the past month has been such a long and difficult one. We will not have to worry about hunger here: the larder is well stocked with groceries brought this morning by Father Bergman. We also have milk cows and a garden from which we will soon be able to harvest.

As promised, Father Bergman gave us a guided tour of the farm. We started with the ancient wooden barn, dark and dingy and seemingly filled to capacity with old hay and manure. In the hay lay pieces of rusty machinery, elaborately draped with layers of delicate cobwebs. I found the cobwebs most intriguing, imagining that they might have been placed there by Mother Nature to afford the machinery some protection against the endless layers of dust that have settled over everything. It is quite obvious that no one has done any serious farming here in some time.

As well, the barn houses seven scrawny cows (mongrel beasts, Gerard disdainfully calls them!), a few chickens, pigs, sheep, two horses and a pony. As we picked our way through the debris underfoot, a few mangy cats quickly scrambled to higher ground from where they hissed out their welcome to us.

Having seen the barn, Father Bergman then led us sheepishly to the potato field which is bearing a meagre crop indeed. The oats field which borders it is sown so thinly that when laying on one's stomach at one end of the field and looking through the stalks of oats, one can see the stand of trees at the other end!

"As I was saying, we are not the greatest farmers," Father spoke in apologetic tones.

On our way to these fields, we crossed a set of railway tracks, thereby solving a mystery which had developed the night before. We had been sleeping peacefully when a thundering roar had awakened us with a start. We lay there, listening to the fearful sound as it continued to build, a furious and terrifying crescendo. "A train?", we had asked each other, thinking that any train this close would surely come right through the house! Then just as quickly it had passed, the roar of the engines wailing in its wake.

With the railway tracks so close to the barnyard, we will have to become accustomed to the comings and goings of the CNR.

The tour completed, Father Bergman suggested that we assume the management of the farm immediately. (I suspect that they may be quite happy to be free of that responsibility!) The farm will continue to supply milk, meat, eggs, potatoes and garden produce to the College and we will be paid one hundred and twenty dollars per month. This is certainly a significant wage increase, for which we are most grateful.

Having said all this, Father climbed into his truck and wished us well. We watched the old truck bump down to the end of the dusty lane where it stopped abruptly, turned a sharp left onto the paved highway, and then accelerated at an alarming rate, the abused engine whining in protest.

We stood in the yard for a moment as the dust settled slowly around us, and studied our new home, its large unpainted wooden mass rising straight and tall from the concrete foundation. There are heaps of scrap wood everywhere, probably left over from when the College was built. The long, narrow, uncurtained windows of the house do not help to soften the picture. Still our soaring spirits are not daunted — there is so much to be done here that we will never have to fear boredom!

The inside of the house is what Gerard calls "rough." Certainly it is very different from the Dutch homes that we have been so used to, but probably quite similar to the wooden structures we see dotted along the roadside here, and similar as well to the Black home. But it is so huge! A large family must have lived here at one time.

The colorless kitchen, for all its size, has only one small cupboard and a shallow enamelled basin situated under a set of taps. The floor, at one time covered with an oilcloth of some sort, now generously shows its planking in many spots. An odd collection of chairs surrounds the long table which has had a piece of vinyl flooring nailed to its top. (The handwork of a practical woman perhaps?) A single bare light bulb, suspended from a frayed, black cord, hangs over the table.

A large wood burning cookstove squats forebodingly at one end of the room, its companion woodbox wedged into the small space behind it. Will I ever learn to use the thing? Playing with fire was never my forte!

There are four doors leading from the kitchen, one to the front hallway, one to the side porch, one to the back shed, and one to the pantry and bathroom. The tiny bathroom situated behind the pantry consists only of a toilet that has been painted a dark green.

Everywhere, the plaster on the walls and ceiling is cracked and flaking. The ceilings are so high that it takes thirteen stair steps to reach the second floor. Throughout the house the wood trim is stained a very dark and sombre color. "Our" bedroom contains a bed and dresser; the other rooms are empty.

This afternoon I unpacked my precious belongings and gave everything a new home. The kitchen table now has a fresh, crisp, cloth cover and a vase of wild flowers as well. The walls are already much friendlier, now adorned with photographs of beloved faces smiling encouragingly at us. It will be so wonderful to clatter my own dishes in my own kitchen as I please! Gerard and I enjoyed our first real "bakje" this evening, although the old stove was none too happy about the prospect of being fired up for a mere cup of coffee!

Tonight we will settle contentedly under our own clean covers on the bed. Gerard promises that we will assemble the bed we have brought with us within a very few days. Although I am filled with excitement I must now try to get some sleep. Tomorrow our hard work will begin in earnest, and I must be ready to rise up to the challenge.

5.

Houseflies and Hardwood Floors

We shall never, ever have reason to be bored here; there is just so much to do! Aside from the regular chores, the milking of the "mongrels" and the feeding of all the animals, Gerard is presently weeding the potato field by hand. At the end of a day's weeding, it is all he can do to make his way painfully and stiffly back to the house. A swim in the nearby creek helps to soothe his aching back though, and the next day he is ready to confront the potato field once more.

The Fathers had a few men employed here but it seems that our exuberance has scared them away permanently. One older man left the day after we arrived — I think that just hearing Gerard's itinerary was too much for him! He had been uncomfortably perched upon one of the many woodpiles, silently observing Gerard literally run from task to task. Finally Gerard strode up to him and asked, "Do you work here?"

"Yep," he responded, his slight frame hunched over a cigarette.

"Good. Let's go to the potato field and start weeding."

"Weeding? How?"

"We'll have to do it by hand."

"Nope."

"No? Don't you work here?"

"Nope. Not any more!" With that he slid stiffly off the woodpile and started down the lane.

The Fathers have gently suggested that perhaps, in our enthusiasm to get things done, we might have been expecting too much from our hired help. That's probably true . . . I guess we must try to adjust to the unhurried "easygoing" nature of our new neighbours. Certainly we don't want to end up ostracizing ourselves. We are different enough already, being the only two pairs of blue eyes in the community!

Today being Sunday, we ventured to the local church where we were greeted with polite handshakes and blatantly curious stares. We must be the very first imports into this small community. During the service, my eyes kept wandering over the little congregation. With their heads bowed low over gnarled hands clutching well-used prayer beads, the members of the congregation all seem to be of similar stature and appearance: of medium height and build, with coarse dark hair, and olive complexions. They do not seem to be a wealthy community; at least we have that in common with them!

Our nearest neighbours are a few fields away, thus leaving us a bit isolated. The Henssons live in a small shack against the woods on our right, and across the fields in the opposite direction are five small homesteads. During the past week the neighbouring menfolk have ambled in and out of the yard, making their acquaintance with Gerard and offering bits of advice. Most of their ramblings he can't understand, but the words, "cold winter," seem to crop up frequently. I cannot imagine that it will ever become as bitterly cold as they (and the Fathers too) seem to be forecasting; the days are so hot and summery right now.

I have yet to meet any of the neighbouring women and I must confess that I am secretly pleased to be left alone for the time being. My English is still so poor, and I am such a faintheart when it comes to trying my hand at it! Gerard and the men ramble on loudly, speaking in fits and starts and all the while gesticulating energetically. I just smile brightly when my presence is acknowledged with a nod or "Hello," and quickly lower my head and resume my work. The visiting men speak so rapidly that even the few words that I so carefully learned while still in Holland, are hopelessly lost in the stacatto rhythm of the conversation!

I have never, in all my days, seen so many houseflies congregate in one house! They are everywhere, clustered in curious patterns on the light bulbs, on the window sills, the ceilings, the kitchen table. Their incessant buzzing and droning is most irritating as they teasingly hover just out of the reach of my one and only inadequate weapon — a yellowed-with-age, rolled-up newspaper. I have had to roll and re-roll the battered paper so many times to avoid smearing the walls with the stains of the casualties (Yes, I do manage to get a few of them!), that the weapon has been reduced to a sticky, broken, shredded mass. Unless I am able to beg, borrow, or purchase a proper fly swatter soon, I fear that we may be chased or carried out of the house by the flies!

Gerard, of course, takes little notice of them. When at lunch, I do constant battle with them, shooing them away from the butter, cheese, jam, and sugar. Gerard's only reaction to their bothersome presence is to occasionally pick up the tattered weapon strategically placed at his elbow, aim, and hit the table with a resounding whack. This usually results in one more casualty and a mildly startled wife! I protest that having the soiled newspaper on the table is less hygienic than having the live flies congregate around us, but Gerard insists that the weapon must be kept close at hand!

Our house is starting to look more presentable — on the inside, that is; the outside remains a mass of dreary unpainted grey. A group of students and their supervisors from the College arrived this past week with the announcement that they were here to clean all of our floors. They brought with them a variety of brooms, mops, soap, rags, and a strange looking machine that is evidently a mechanized cleaner of some sort. Curious but wanting to stay out of their way, I observed from a distance as they tackled the task enthusiastically. (I hazard a guess that for the boys, a day away from the College is a welcome holiday, even if that day is spent washing floors elsewhere!)

It quickly became apparent that the modern-looking machine was no match for the age-old grime tenaciously adhered to the hardwood floors. Consequently it was soon abandoned in favor of scrub brushes and hot, soapy water. All around me were young boys on hands and knees scrubbing vigorously, other boys struggling with oversized mops and trying to control the excess water that was seeping everywhere, and still another crew busily engaged on the "rinse" patrol.

In one of the bedrooms the vigorous scrubbing loosened grain after grain of oats which had been concealed in the tiny crevices between the narrow floorboards. One of the supervisors explained that this room had, until recently, been used as a grainery for a number of years. Small wonder that we have a rodent problem!

With the task finally completed, tools were collected and pails of blackened water were emptied into a nearby ditch. As the group departed with our thanks echoing in their ears, a blanket of quiet settled over the house once more. It had been most consoling to listen to the cheerful banter of the young voices, their chatter richly interspersed with high-pitched peals of laughter. I hope that some day the laughter of our own children will fill these rooms with warmth and richness. This house is entirely too big for the two of us.

We have been doing some 'redecorating!' Our own bed has been assembled and installed into the little room above the kitchen. The other bed has been moved into the adjacent room, now dubbed our 'guestroom.'

(And, wonder of wonders, we will soon have our very first overnight guests. My newly married sister, Gonda, and her husband, Marinus, will be stopping over to visit with us on their way from Holland to their future home in California. Before we had left Holland, Gonda had casually mentioned the possibility of a visit; now, a recently arrived telegram has confirmed their plans. Seeing Gonda again is something I look forward to with all my heart. Her presence will be tangible proof that my precious Home still does exist, although it feels as if I have not been there in many, many years.)

To return to our decorating, Gerard has built a small shelf in the kitchen on which I can display some of my beloved collectibles — a wooden shoe, a cheery teapot, a small ceramic windmill, and more photographs in stand-up frames, all placed on little lace doilies. The colorful, woven "wandoek" which hangs above the shelf does much to add to the coziness. We seem to spend much of our time in the kitchen; the other rooms are so bleak and empty.

Our meals are simple but nourishing. There are always potatoes and fresh vegetables from the garden. Sometimes we are fortunate to have a piece of meat, and often we enjoy a custard for dessert. Every morning Gerard fires up the old sloth-of-a-stove, and I roll up my sleeves in preparation to do battle with it. My confidence in dealing with the beast is invariably always shattered as lids steam off pots and water sputters everywhere, or dinner stubbornly refuses to boil, merely sitting there in lukewarm water or gravy. Thank heaven for that old standby, lettuce and mayonnaise!

Doing the laundry constitutes the making of another adventure. I had been washing our clothes by hand when the Fathers put forth a proposal that I have eagerly accepted. Once a week I and my laundry will be chauffeured to the College where I will do their washing as well as ours, using their modern equipment. As well, on 'wash day," Gerard and I will have our supper with the Fathers. This added bonus might well end up becoming our best meal of the week!

On my first washday, I was shown the laundry facilities by a lady from the neighbourhood who is evidently a housekeeper at the College. She introduced herself as Beatrice and resumed her duties as I prepared to tackle a formidable pile of laundry.

Periodically she would reappear, asking if I wished to use what I understood to be the bedroom. Thinking that she thought that I would perhaps like to break for a short nap, I replied that I was not tired. This scenario was repeated a number of times, leaving me increasingly puzzled. Finally she appeared once more, took me by the hand and led me firmly but gently to . . . the bathroom!

"Oh, thank you!", I exclaimed, grateful for the opportunity to use the facility. We exchanged bright smiles and she continued on her way. As for me, I've taken another tiny step towards being 'Canadianized!'

6.

Samaritans in Black

Our visitors have come and gone, their presence having offered a comforting but brief sojourn from all that is so new and unfamiliar here. How Gonda and I chatted on and on while we worked, strolled through the pastures, or simply sat in the yard. My tongue eagerly wrapped itself around the dear, Dutch language and my heart ached hungrily for yet more news from home.

"Tell me again how Vader and Moeder are."

All too soon the visit came to an end. While waiting for the train that would carry them far away, I squeezed back the tears and hugged my sister tightly. When will I see her again?

Another precious letter arrived from Overseas today, resplendent with the sights, sounds, and even the familiar smells of my beloved Homeland. This, coupled with my already acute sense of loneliness was too much for my composure. I must confess that I was severely struck with an unexpected bout of homesickness, momentarily allowing myself to wallow in bitter tears of self-pity.

Enough of this blatant self-indulgence, however! We must be most thankful for what we have — each other, an income, and a home with a telephone, electricity, running water, and toilet facilities. According to the Fathers, our humble little green toilet is a luxury that many people in the community are still doing without. As if to verify this, an outhouse stands mere yards from the house, tall and arched slightly backward like a proud and silent sentinel ready to resume its duty, should this ever become necessary!

The Fathers, good samaritans in black, are being most wonderful to us. I dread to think what we would do without them. We are able to buy our groceries from them at wholesale cost and often they bring leftover food from the cafeteria, which we gratefully accept. Daily they come to collect milk, cream, eggs and produce, and often they leave behind buckets of potato peels and vegetable scraps for the pigs.

On one of their most recent visits, the Fathers brought with them some new tenants for us — one hundred baby chicks cleverly disguised by Mother Nature as yellow balls of fluff. We quickly decided on the ideal spot for raising chicks past their precarious babyhood — the former grainery, also known as the recently scrubbed bedroom.

Why not, I thought as brooders, feeders, and heat lamps were being noisily assembled. We certainly don't need that room and besides, the chicks will be close at hand for feeding. Who knows, perhaps they might even complete the task of coaxing the last few grains of oats from between the floor boards!

I've discovered a rather effective way to keep the flies at bay! I now cover the plate of bread, the butter dish, and the cheese with bowls turned upside down. Of course the flies still land on our plates as we butter bread and make our sandwiches, but at least I no longer have to contend with the disdainful task of gingerly picking struggling flies out of the butter dish.

I have also acquired a fly swatter — from the College, of course! Gerard's aim with it is quite deadly. Thank heaven the thing is washable!

The Fathers travel to 'town' on a regular basis to order or buy supplies and to conduct various other business there. Town is either Bathurst or Dalhousie, each being about an hour's drive from here. Often they stop by to see if there is anything they can bring back for us and occasionally they invite us along. On his last trip to town, Gerard purchased a small hot plate which he presented to me with a triumphant grin on his face!

The making of our bakje this evening was executed with such flair and ease! I could almost imagine the stodgy wood stove heaving a sleepy sigh of relief as I placed the kettle on the hot plate. The preparation of meals will be so much easier now, leaving time for the many other tasks that abound.

We have finished bringing in the hay, meagre crop that it is. Gerard has mowed every blade of grass there is and the sum total of all these blades will have to see the animals through the winter. Next year we hope to seed a decent crop, perhaps even adding some fertilizer if the Fathers agree.

The process of harvesting the hay is much the same here as it is in Holland, except that here we have less manpower and a tractor instead of horses. I was appointed to drive the tractor, a rusty old 'Cockshutt 60,' but aside from posing momentarily behind the wheel for a few hurried photographs, I did not endeavor to do much driving. I have never been able to derive much pleasure from nervous horses and noisy machinery and am pleased to leave well enough alone in both categories!

Soon we will be harvesting the grain and potato crops from those forlorn fields behind the railway tracks. Hopefully there will be enough potatoes for the College and for ourselves too, to see us all through the winter.

My beloved and I have been harbouring a very special secret these past few days. It seems that we are going to become parents in about six or seven months time. No, I have not had this medically confirmed. Where would I go? What would I say? I hardly know how to ask for a bowl of soup in English, never mind trying to explain that I think I am 'in verwachting!' However, the signs and symptoms of pregnancy are all there.

Yes, the priceless little rose within me has brought a tiny thorn or two. My stomach has been behaving miserably this last week, reminiscent of my stormy passage mere months ago. I am trying to defy the queasiness by being outdoors as much as possible and forcing the fresh clean air deeply into my lungs. Eating has once again become an arduous trial. Sometimes I run to the shore of the bay, mere minutes away, in an attempt to escape the food odors that permeate my kitchen. Even there, where the ocean tides caress the warm sand which in turn nuzzles the tufts of crabgrass that venture to grow on the edge of the beach, my nausea envelops me like a dark, stifling cloak.

Aside from this temporary difficulty, we are elated to be welcoming a baby into our little family. I can hardly wait to hold and cherish this beloved bundle, this Canadian child of ours who will know this community and this country as his home.

Gerard will be a good and proud father, an unfailing provider for his family. Already he is bursting with pride, still not quite able to believe that a child of ours will soon be born.

Although I am greatly tempted to write of this wonderful news to our parents, I must refrain from doing so until we are more certain that all will go well with the pregnancy. At the moment we are sharing this secret with no one, not even the Fathers. However, if I don't soon regain my appetite, even they, men of the cloth who are generally ill at ease with such worldly affairs as having a baby, will begin to wonder about my condition!

The days are steadily getting shorter and the evenings have developed a crisp coolness not noticed before. The evening skies are often breathtaking, with bands of blood-red light lavishly painted along the western horizon. I was most astonished recently to notice that our green trees are actually changing color. Thinking that I must be imagining this unfamiliar phenomenon, I examined the trees more closely and, sure enough, noticed the first hints of gold, orange and even crimson on the delicate leaves.

What a wonderfully strange country this is, with its untiring variety of natural marvels to render me awestruck! The forests of Holland are so small, so planned, so predictable, green in the summer and, except for the evergreens, bare and drab in the winter. Here, I feel as if I am about to witness the unfolding of a marvelous profusion of colour, one last brash display to delight the senses before the onset of a long, hard winter.

I must now brace myself, hold my nose, and attempt to prepare a meal. Although I know that I will not be eating anything, there is a hungry man roaming around outdoors who will soon be anticipating the call to supper!

7.

Medical Complications

I have spent the last agonizingly long ten days in hospital, praying that I will not lose this precious life within me. I am surrounded by bare, pale green walls, coarse white linen, and people who chatter on in a language that I still don't really understand at all.

Prior to being hospitalized, I had not eaten for days and had felt gravely ill and alarmingly weak. However, Gerard and I had been determined to struggle through this ordeal on our own. I, for one, did not relish the thought of being delivered into the hands of a strange physician in such an alien environment as a hospital! In Holland, the physician makes house calls and the patient is coaxed back to health at her home, by her own family. Here it seems that one is dropped off, alone, at the hospital, where one must take leave of one's family and be content to see them only during specified visiting periods.

For weeks I had been steadily losing weight and could see no improvement in my poor state of health. One day, one of the Fathers had somberly remarked to Gerard:

"Jane seems very sick. I think we should take her to the hospital."

For the sake of our baby, I had unwillingly allowed

myself to be taken to the hospital in Campbellton, a small city some forty-five miles away. The Fathers had arranged for me to be examined by Dr. Dumas, their 'family' physician there, and as usual they had provided transportation. Tightly wedged between Gerard and the chauffeur in the tiny cab of the truck, and clutching a plastic bag intended to catch the curdled contents of my mutinous stomach, we had bumped along the highway, mile after merciless mile.

When we had finally arrived at the hospital, I had been almost beyond the point of really caring what would become of me.

But you must care, I had kept admonishing myself sternly. For the sake of the baby, you must not stop caring!

With Gerard and the chauffeur left behind in the waiting area to explain my ailment to the admitting staff, I was briskly wheeled upstairs and assigned to a narrow metal bed in a large dormitory. I was helped into bed and brought a bedpan which I immediately put to good use, retching loudly and spasmodically.

A short time later, Gerard tiptoed into the room, cautiously taking in his antiseptic surroundings. When he caught sight of me in my little corner of the large room, he hurried over and embraced me for a long moment.

"You must stay here for a few days. They are worried about the baby and about the weight that you have been losing. Don't worry," he smiled bravely. "As soon as you can keep down some food, they will let you come home. It will only be for a few days."

After a moment of silence, he continued quietly, "I must go now. I can't keep the driver waiting much longer. I promise that I will visit soon. I'm sure the Fathers will bring me as often as they can."

He kissed me and held me tightly.

"Be good!", he finally said, winking at me mischieviously. "Don't talk the doctor's ear off!" With that, he walked across the room and lingered briefly in the doorway to glance back at me sadly.

"It will be lonely at home without you," he spoke softly, shaking his head forlornly. And then he was gone, leaving me to cope with this new and uneasy environment.

When the physician finally arrived, he examined me quickly, all-the-while smiling and nodding encouragingly. He spoke a few short sentences that I failed to understand and hastily exited the room.

Shortly thereafter, a nurse arrived with a large jar of white intravenous liquid which she efficiently proceeded to connect to my arm. As well, she administered a medication which she loudly and slowly proclaimed was 'for your stomach,' pointing to my abdomen for added emphasis.

My routine these past ten days has largely revolved around the intravenous and medication schedules, occasionally interspersed with a bowl of chicken soup which the nurses cajole me into eating. I always oblige, but the soup usually ends up splattered ungraciously into a nearby bedpan.

Unless I succeed in keeping some food down, I will probably stay here, hooked up to these dreaded tubes, until the baby is born. Oh God, no, please, I want to go home, to my own little nest where I can be more content than I will ever be here! I must try harder to eat, to keep the food down.

My roommates here have been friendly enough, but with no one to talk to, I am getting very depressed and lonely. Gerard comes to visit every few days, and I cling to him as I cling to the minutes that tick by on the clock, dreading that inevitable moment he must dejectedly announce his departure.

'My' physician seems concerned about the baby, which, of course, is no consolation to me. He examines me daily, listening carefully for a tiny heartbeat and frowning deeply all the while. When he catches me staring questioningly at him, he quickly smoothes the furrows in his brow, pats my arm and tries to reassure me.

What is he thinking? I have a hundred questions for him and I need to know desperately that this baby will be fine. Father Bergman, where are you when I really need you? Lord, could you send him to me just one more time? Tonight I must really pray fervently that the Lord will see us through all of this. He must know how much we need this baby!

I spend the long hours reading and re-reading letters from Home and the one precious magazine that Gerard brought with him on his last visit. It arrived in the mail recently, a thoughtful gift from his parents. He presented it to me unopened, even though I knew that he must have longed to read it himself first. Such a wonderfully considerate husband I have! How dare I feel sorry for myself!

Our secret is still intact, although I long to write a lengthy letter to my mother and lift the burden of secrecy from my shoulders. She would understand how anxious I feel about this baby . . . and yet, she must not know until this danger has passed. Our families must be spared the worry that they would surely suffer if they knew of our current situation.

Our parents and families have been so supportive in their many wonderful and uplifting letters. Each precious, pale blue, air-mail envelope comes filled with delicious news from family and community. Each letter is digested silently, recited aloud, read, re-read, and finally tucked away for safekeeping.

Outside, dusk is falling rapidly and an angry wind is whipping at the cowering, nearly bare trees. How lonely and vulnerable they look now, stripped of their magnificent cloaks of green. Heavy swollen clouds are furling and unfurling in the greying sky. There will be rain tonight.

Down the hall I hear the clatter of supper trays being noisily distributed. Tonight I must will myself, force myself, to eat and to keep my food down. I am absolutely disgusted with my stomach, miserable and rebellious beast that it has been! Tonight I eat and that is that!

8.

The Rat-Infested Furnace

I and the resilient little being within me have been returned safely to our home, and to our own life. Even this drafty old cavern of a house with its flaking ceilings and imposing woodwork is a most welcome and comforting sight after my long absence!

We are indebted to Providence for seeing us all safely through this ordeal. Although I was most anxious to leave the hospital and did not enjoy my two-week stay there, I admit that I owe the life of my tiny developing offspring, and perhaps my own life as well, to the care that I received there.

I am managing to eat, and even to keep the precious nourishment down, although mealtime remains an ordeal. I am rapidly falling into the habit of nibbling a bit here and there, rather than eating full meals. My stomach seems to prefer that arrangement, and the constant uprisings within me are finally beginning to subside.

It is wonderful to be home again! The days are becoming much colder now, and the rainy days seem especially chilling. We are spending all of our free time gathering firewood from the wooded area beyond the railway tracks. We are especially careful to gather every little stick of wood we find, for we know that any green wood that has to be cut to complete our winter's supply will not provide much heat.

Each day we set out after lunch with our one horse, Prince, harnessed to an awkward looking cart with oversized wooden wheels. I, armed with an assortment of little snacks, usually choose to stroll behind the squeaking, plodding, cortege. Once near the woods, we work steadily, collecting every twig and branch that we find. Using a small hatchet, Gerard deftly chops the cumbersome pieces into sticks of a more manageable size.

By mid-afternoon, we return home with a cart full of precious dry wood which we proceed to toss into the basement of the house. I enjoy these outings so, working side by side with my love and laughing and chattering all the while.

Prince, our good-humoured horse, endures our doings obediently and patiently. I suspect that he might even enjoy these excursions, stopping occasionally for an unhurried nibble of tender vegetation. Tall, pure-white, and graceful, he is a handsome and endearing fellow. Gerard guesses that he is at least twenty years old, which makes him a very old horse. I wonder how long he has lived here, and where he came from. Surely he is not an ordinary work horse, with his gentle, intelligent eyes and proud carriage. Perhaps some day we will find out more about him.

An assessment of our heating system has left Gerard concerned. Our furnace, disfigured piece of metal that it is, is filled with gaping holes and has for some time served as a nesting area for a sizable colony of rodents. The pipes are rotting; a gentle tap against them produces an ominous cloud of blended fine, red dust and black soot.

It looks like we'll have to depend on our kitchen stove for heat. Its piping is not much better, but with a little luck, it will see us through the winter.

I have already put extra blankets on the bed, and we have started lighting the stove in the evening. Mornings are cold but once the sleepy stove is again roused, warmth and comfort prevail in the kitchen at least. I really cannot envision that it will get much colder, and surely the month of March will bring spring once again!

We had a brief snowfall in late October and one of our

neighbours had then suggested that the cows be brought from the pasture and stabled for the winter. Surely the snow will go away and the animals can stay out for another month, we had reasoned. That snow did melt, but the weather has become entirely too inclement for these spiritless, lowly beasts. Consequently, they have been relegated to their dark little stalls for the winter.

It seems that we have much to learn about the Canadian winter!

We have embarked on a new venture, one that is essential to our becoming properly Canadianized, but leaves us exhausted and drained from the effort. A few weeks ago, one of the Fathers, Father Mario, proposed that he teach us to speak English. After our ordeal with my hospitalization, and realizing the serious implications of not being able to speak the language of the land, we readily agreed.

Fortunately, we had thought to bring from Holland the books and material we had used in a short course on the English language while still in Holland. We are being tutored two evenings a week without fail. Although Father speaks no Dutch and we little English, he is a marvellous teacher and we are really learning!

The English have a mysterious way of contorting the tongue to produce a delicate, whispery sound, best described on paper as simply, "th." Although I am managing to reproduce this sound with some accuracy, Gerard seems hopelessly tongue-tied. As I try not to giggle and Father staves off the smiles that rise within him, Gerard painstakingly goes through the incantation: THese . . . THose . . . THem . . . THere.

"Don't worry, Gerard," Father then says with a chuckle as Gerard sits shaking his head, "Women just have a sharper tongue for this sort of thing! Keep trying and you will learn!"

When the lesson comes to an end, we invariably always fall into bed, totally exhausted. Will we ever learn to master this complex, alien language?

Our other evenings are spent writing letters, reading the magazines that now arrive on a regular basis, or playing cards. When we occasionally venture to practise our English, we more often than not end up gently teasing each other's mispronunciations. Our tutor would not find us too productive on our own, I am afraid!

Within the next few weeks, I will have to begin preparing for the Feast of Sint Nicolaas which, I have been told by the Fathers, is not observed in Canada. In Holland, gifts are exchanged on this day, good food is enjoyed, and the merrymaking abounds. In contrast, the Dutch Christmas is largely a religious feast, observed by attending church and spending the day quietly with family and friends. Here, it seems that all of the feasting and gifting is enjoyed on Christmas day.

We must try very hard not to succumb to loneliness and depression during this season. Our families are always in our hearts, but especially during the month of December we will be thinking about them, longing to be with them. We must not think about the feasting and the family gatherings that will surely be taking place in our little hometowns.

This is our home now. This is where our unborn child will belong.

Lately I have had a persistent craving for Dutch foods, especially cheese. The cheese here is so different, so bland. Perhaps one day I will get used to it. Perhaps I will even taste the wonderful sharpness of Gouda again some distant day!

9.

Sint Nicolaas & Christmas

December has been a month filled with learning experiences. Admittedly, we seem to have spent much of it torn between our loyalty to cherished Dutch traditions on the one hand, and, on the other, trying to understand the new and unfamiliar customs that are observed here. Lest I leave the impression that we have ventured into the community to 'observe' the festive customs of our neighbours, let me hasten to add that we remain securely isolated on our farm, busy with our chores which must all be done by hand, and confined by the cold and chilling weather that we have been experiencing. As well, our limited English continues to keep us, especially me, from venturing boldly and confidently into the community!

My preparations for our Sint Nicolaas celebration on December 5 included instances of both frustration and humour. Filled with visions of the grand pastries and delicious cakes that are the trademark of the splendid pastry shops in Holland, I embarked enthusiastically on my very first 'Canadian' baking spree. With my sleeves rolled up and my one Dutch cookbook close at hand, I energetically measured and weighed the flour, sugar, and butter. I hummed absent-mindedly while I worked, ignoring the squeals of protest from the old rusty weigh scale that Gerard had found in the barn.

"I'm not sure this will work," Gerard mused over my shoulder. "I think that our pound is actually heavier than the English pound. This business about sixteen ounces has me somewhat confused."

And so, on the advice of my husband, I started improvising: a pound of flour now became 'a pound and a bit.' With grandiose visions of delectable delights beginning to fade, I tersely added the milk and the eggs, beating the suffering batter with growing annoyance.

A quick search of the pantry produced a grimy and dented cakepan of the wrong dimension, which nonetheless would have to do. After a thorough scrubbing such as the pan had probably not beheld in years, the batter was finally ready for the oven.

Therein lay my next obstacle: this oven's thermostat uses a system of measurement that is totally alien to me, something called 'fahrenheit.' My recipe directed that I set my oven to 'Propane No. 6!' Exasperated, I threw an extra log into the firebox, and roughly slid the pan into the oven. I briskly clapped the cookbook shut, little clouds of flour dust rising from its pages, and relegated it to an obscure corner of the pantry.

How do Canadian women bake, I kept asking myself as I tidied the counter. They must use a different system which means that, until I learn to decipher an English cookbook, I might as well abandon my aspiration to produce some decent home baking.

Thank heaven old Mrs. Black taught me to bake bread. Like her, I don't measure anything, just adding flour until the dough is light and kneadable. I make sure the oven is hot but pay no attention to the 'fahrenheits'!

As I had feared, the cake cooperated miserably by refusing to rise, settling heavily and firmly on the bottom of the pan instead. When it was finally made to budge, it came out of the pan in hard, inedible-looking pieces.

"It's not bad," Gerard said encouragingly as he crunched loudly and laboriously on a charred morsel. "Perhaps the oven was just a bit too hot!"

Our second venture in preparation for Sint Nicolaas involved a trip to town with the Fathers. Like excited youngsters, we strolled along the main street and gazed into the little storefront windows at the sights of the season. At a pastry shop, we allowed ourselves to enter and choose a treat from the glass display case. Our selection was based solely on appearance, for we had no idea what these foreign delights would taste like, nor dared we to ask.

In a department store, we separated momentarily to secretly purchase a small trinket for each other. Together again, we selected an inexpensive set of Christmas figurines, delicate ceramic replicas of the Christ child and Mother, Joseph, the shepherds, kings and one camel. It is comforting to know that the wonderfully familiar Christmas story is an integral part of Christmas in this country as well.

Our next stop was the grocer where we bought some special treats that would constitute our festive meal. I searched in vain for worst, Dutch cheese, and Dutch soups and custards. Instead we settled for a tin of meat called "corned beef" — the taste is new to us but not bad. We also bought a package of fancy looking cookies which turned out to be a disappointment. A bag of plump juicy oranges completed our expedition.

In high spirits and laden with the fruits of our outing, we returned at lunchtime to find the house without a trace of heat. Shivering uncontrollably and with my coat still on, I hurriedly made some sandwiches while Gerard roused the sluggish stove back to life. Still shivering, we huddled over the stove, hesitant to leave the heat even for the plates of sandwiches that beckoned from the kitchen table.

"I really think that the temperature in here is below freezing point," Gerard remarked, observing a powdery dusting of ice glisten along the ceiling of the outside wall.

"I have an idea," he suddenly added. "Let's pull the wood box away from behind the stove and we can slide a little table and two chairs in that space. Then we can eat our lunch in comfort."

Quickly we coaxed the wood box from its warm refuge and replaced it with a tottery little table and two chairs. Tightly wedged between the stove and the wall, we were finally ready to enjoy our meal.

"You can take your mittens off now," Gerard teased

smilingly as I hugged myself in an attempt to feel warm. Famished, we delved into our sandwiches with great enthusiasm and savored every drop of the piping hot coffee.

Suddenly, without warning, a quick loud bang reverberated through the kitchen, causing us to startle and look at each other questioningly. After a brief moment, Gerard started to smile.

"Do you know what it was?", I asked anxiously.

"I believe," he said slowly, his smile widening, "that our little green toilet has just exploded."

We rushed through the pantry and into the tiny bathroom. There lay the humiliated toilet, its china bowl erupted into three irrepairable segments. In the centre of this arrangement lay the culprit, a huge block of ice that had once been merely benign water in the bowl. When the temperature in the house had started to drop, the water in the toilet had frozen, creating an immense pressure against the bowl. Finally the toilet had reluctantly succumbed to the forces of nature!

My reaction should have been one of dismay, and instead I started to giggle uncontrollably!

"Let's finish lunch first," Gerard suggested, still smiling. "We can leave the ice here too, for now. We don't have to worry about it melting!" As he spoke, his breath rose up to the ceiling in moist white puffs.

Thanks to the Fathers, the toilet was replaced within the week, but not after many frigid trips to the barn to answer Nature's call! I never realized that Nature called quite this often, especially during pregnancy!

A parcel arrived from Home just in time for Sint Nicolaas Day. Excitedly I tore away the layers of brown paper to reveal an aromatic collection of the festive foods for which we had been craving! How good it was to feast my eyes upon the speculaas, a spicy gingerbread in the shape of Sint Nic himself, the chocolates and cocoa, the hagelslaag and butter cake, and of course the letters and cards from every member of the family.

How we read and re-read their greetings as we savoured a cup of hot cocoa and a piece of speculaas. How we laughed at ourselves as we observed the Dutch tradition of setting out our "klompen" filled with straw, for the good Sint's horse. How misty our eyes grew as we talked of bygone holidays and reminisced about the family gatherings that we had once so taken for granted.

Christmas Day brought a light dusting of snow that fell to the muddy ground like powdered sugar carelessly strewn on the top of an undercooked chocolate cake. At church we lost ourselves in the cherished Christmas hymns, relishing the familiarity of the music and forgetting momentarily that the words were alien to us.

The wonderful Fathers visited in the afternoon, bringing a bountious gift of food with them. As well, two youngsters from the neighbourhood struggled up the muddy lane to offer us a basket of food that had been prepared by their mother. Gratefully we accepted their gift and invited the children to stay for hot cocoa and cookies.

Finally, the company having parted and the tedious barn chores completed, we enjoyed a quiet evening meal together and observed our peaceful surroundings with contentment. The supper table was laden with a wonderful assortment of bread, sweets, ham, and cheese. On a side table stood our tree, a small fir decorated with ornaments made out of the foil paper found in cigarette packages, and with tiny knick-knacks from around the house. Beneath the tree stood a creche, lovingly made by Gerard out of birch branches and the wood of an old orange crate. In it were nestled the reverent figurines, serenely grouped around the manger containing the Child.

Yes, it has been a good Christmas for us. Although far from our own dear families and friends, we have been shown much kindness by the people here and are grateful to them. It is so comforting to know that we are among good and decent people.

And so we start 1953 with our spirits solidly intact. A precious child will soon be born, and the Fathers continue to keep us under their wing. We have truly been blessed with good fortune!

10.

Winter's Icy Grip

Nothing could have adequately prepared us for the amount of snow that has fallen from the sky in the last few weeks. On New Year's day it began to snow — softly, gently, hypnotically, reticent of the furious storm that was about to be unleashed. We gazed with wonder through the frost-tinged windows at the landscape which was being steadily and completely transformed into a pristine world of glistening white. Awestruck, we stared at the row of fence posts that stood like rigid sentinels, attired in new busbies of powdery white. Even the trees have been transformed, taking on an air of resignation and reluctantly submitting to the unwieldy burden of snow on branches and boughs.

And then the wind came. Through the trees it roared and dipped, unyielding in its rage and fury. Again and again it attacked the side of the house, causing the old structure to quiver under the impact. Gusting, swelling, and subsiding but for a moment, it swept the snow into huge drifts against the house.

Even inside, the ruthlessness of the wind could be felt. Icy, drafty fingers of pure cold seeped in around the door and window frames, bringing sudden puffs of powdery snow which settled, unmelted, onto the floor. The ill-fitting window panes rattled noisily in their frames, threatening to shatter with every unrelentless blast.

The inadequacy of our heating system now began to dawn more fully on us; all day we huddled over the stove, dressed in layers of clothing, woolen socks and our "klompen." Even as the fire roared and the pipes began to glow ominously, the kitchen remained cold and drafty.

By mid-afternoon Gerard ventured to the barn to start the daily ritual of cleaning, feeding, and milking that awaited him there. Through the heavily frosted window, I watched him struggle through the snow drifts, leaning into the merciless wind with hands and ears exposed to the cruel elements. Finally, after what seemed like an eternity, he reached the barn door, struggled momentarily to open it, and disappeared quickly into the warm haven inside.

Upon his return, I was shocked to see him so totally covered with snow. It clung tenaciously to his hair, was packed solidly down his neck and up his pant legs against clammy, bluish skin, and had even crept up his sleeves and into his ears.

"I've never seen anything like this," he declared, struggling to take off his snow-filled boots. "Surely we've had half a meter already, and there is no sign of the storm letting up."

All night it continued, slamming furious gusts of wind against the moaning, creaking house. Huddled under the blankets and coats which we had piled on top of the bed, we finally fell asleep to the howling crescendo of the wind and the incessant rattle of the window panes.

In the morning, the house was colder than any cold I had ever experienced before. The kitchen was dusted with a fine layer of powdery snow that had been swept in through the many cracks. The stove, stone-cold hunk of iron that it was, grudgingly submitted to yet another roaring fire in its firebox. Shivering, we dressed quickly in front of the stove, warming our hands on the blackened pipe.

"Somehow, I think that most of the precious heat is going up the chimney," I observed as the pipes rapidly warmed while the stove itself still remained cool.

Gerard nodded in agreement, munching on a piece of

dry bread. Steaming coffee, made on the hot plate, never tasted so good!

After breakfast, we donned many layers of clothing and ventured outdoors to view the new and alien panorama of winter. The wind had finally abated and the sun shone brilliantly, filling the pure crystals of snow with such intense light that one had to squint to protect the eyes. We had never seen this much brightness before; the sky was a pure brilliant blue and the snow a flawless, sparkling, dancing white. Everywhere, delicately carved drifts of snow lay unfurled, their graceful curves and shapes reminiscent of gentle ocean waves.

I looked skyward and breathed deeply, emitting the cold air in gasps. After being confined to the dimly lit kitchen for the past twenty-four hours, all this brightness and freshness felt so good!

We ventured towards the barn, searching in vain for a trace of the tracks Gerard had made the day before. Now I experienced a sensation that was totally new to me: that of cold, unmelting snow pressed mercilessly against my stockinged legs. As we trudged, my low unlined boots filled and overflowed with snow which first chilled, then burned, and finally numbed my exposed skin.

In the dimly lit barn, we shook ourselves vigorously and emptied our boots of packed snow. Without removing any clothing, we set about the morning's chores. A warm, musky steam emanated from the animals as they happily munched on hay and oats. When Gerard threw open the barn door to heave out the steaming manure from the stables, a frosty layer of ice settled on the tender wet muzzles of the cows and their hair became matted with glistening crystals of snow.

We poured the pails of milk into a can which we placed in a corner of the little milk shed, hoping that it wouldn't freeze there and yet not daring to store it in the warmth of the barn. Later that day, once the highway had been ploughed clear of snow, Gerard would hitch Prince to the old bobsled and venture to the end of the lane with the milk where it would be loaded onto the Fathers' truck.

Prince and that sled have been our lifeline to the Fathers, bringing groceries and feed for the animals, and carrying out cans of milk for the College. With his massive shoulders against the harness and with head lowered to the wind, Prince plods obediently up and down the lane pulling the tedious sled behind him. Sometimes the freshly fallen snow is so deep that he struggles along perilously, his head bobbing up and down from the effort. Gerard never hurries him, letting the reins lie slack on his rump, and clucking encouragingly to him all the while. Invariably the trip back to the stable is always completed in less time than the trip out!

Our days are spent in isolation for even the Fathers have ceased to visit until the weather becomes a bit more hospitable. Looking across the snow-covered fields we see curly wisps of smoke rising from the little group of houses on the horizon; our neighbours too, seem to be surviving the winter.

We always look forward to our only weekly outing — attending church on Sunday morning. We hitch Prince to the sled and make our way to the home of one of the neighbours who takes us to church in his truck for a fee of ten cents. Meanwhile, Prince waits obediently by the roadside.

It has become most obvious to us that we were very ill-prepared for this Canadian winter. Never did we imagine that there would be this much snow. Indeed, with all of the Canadian promotional material that we viewed while still in Holland, we can't recall seeing a single slide or photograph of snow.

Our clothing is so woefully inadequate. Our only footwear are Dutch wooden 'klompen' and low unlined leather walking boots, with neither zipper nor laces to shut out the snow. We have no long underwear nor tights. By the Grace of God I have one pair of slacks; slacks for women had just appeared on the market in Holland and a thinking relative had urged me to take along a pair. I wear those slacks every day over my pajamas and with at least two pairs of woolen socks!

Our cloth coats are hoodless, thin and unlined, hardly a match for the cruel merciless winds. We have scarves and a pair of mittens each, but no caps and no heavy sweaters. We know that we will have to make do with what we have for there is so little money to spend. Much of our precious savings was used to pay for my recent hospitalization, and more will have to be spent when the time arrives for our baby to be born.

The kitchen remains a cold, dimly lit cavern. Outside the snow is piled in hard, dense drifts that reach almost to the top of the windows. Much as we would enjoy sunlight streaming through the kitchen windows, we are hesitant to remove the snow that must surely be helping to insulate this old house.

There are days when I just cannot get warm. I try to keep myself busy in the kitchen, wearing my usual layers of clothing and sometimes my mittens as well. Trips to the toilet are quick and only when absolutely necessary; severe frostbite is always an imminent danger!

Our stove and its paraphernalia of piping is a genuine fire hazard, but we are forced to either use it or freeze. When the fire is at its hottest, which means that one can feel the heat radiating a mere meter away from the stove, the pipe glows a dull orange through the three stories of this old wooden structure. Given half a chance, this house would burn to a cinder with little coaxing!

At night we huddle under the mound of blankets on our bed and let the fire die. It would be much too hazardous to keep more than a hot coal or two untended in the firebox.

And always, we keep saying to each other, "Surely spring cannot be much further away!" Our words drift off as we stare out of the window at the endless layers of snow. The silent, rigid banks seem to admonish our foolish hopes, their imposing stature exuding their intention to extend the winter as long as possible.

A few days ago the waterline that runs from the house to the barn froze, thereby cutting off the entire water supply to the animals. Left with no other choice, we proceeded to shovel a narrow path from the house to the barn, inching our way through the hard-packed snow. When that gruesome task was finally completed, we placed an old metal washtub just outside of the porch door and filled it with buckets of water from the tap in the kitchen. Then we untied the cows and led them, one by one, out of the barn and up the path to the tub. Needing no further coaxing, they drank noisily and unhurriedly, their velvety muzzles seemingly afloat upon the icy water while clouds of dank moist steam rose slowly from their flanks.

Prince and the pony are watered this way as well. We carry pails of water to the pigs and sheep, foolish beasts that would become hopelessly entangled in the drifts of snow. This entire watering procedure is repeated twice daily and will probably have to be continued until the ground thaws in spring.

Spring will not come soon enough for me. How I will rejoice when I see the first tender new buds on the trees, the first fragile blades of grass peering through the snow. Our families must shake their heads when they read our vivid descriptions of winter, wondering what has given way to our seemingly unrestrained bouts of exaggeration. Not until they actually see this will they really believe it!

Oh, Spring, where are you? Are you watching the wrath of winter from a safe distance? I await your arrival impatiently for I am beginning to fear that I may never feel warm again. Come and deliver me from the icy, deathly grip of winter!

11.

Snowshoes & Baby Things

February has literally been the longest, darkest month of my life! The snow drifts against the windows have succeeded in blocking out most of the daylight, and the single bare bulb suspended over the kitchen table remains lit all day long. Even then, eerie shadows creep along the ceiling, and darkness constantly lurks in the far corners of the room.

I am sitting on a chair in front of the stove with my feet propped upon the open oven door. I think my toes are finally beginning to thaw! With my coat wrapped snugly around my shoulders, I sit staring at the growing roundness that is slowly taking over the space that was once my lap. Don't rush to be born, Little One, for where you are now is a much more agreeable environment than the one into which you are soon to enter.

The highlight of this month was the arrival of a large parcel from my mother which was filled to repletion with 'baby things.' Oh, you wonderful, resourceful, dear mother, I thought as I lifted item after marvellous item out of the box. First came the baby clothes, the undershirts and diapers, the knitwear, the stockings, and bonnets. Next came blankets, sheets and embroidered pillowcases. These were followed by two metal hot water bottles and an assortment of baby bath products.

Finally, at the bottom of the box, lay an unassembled wicker bassinet complete with mattress and hood, and lined with a luxuriously lustrous satin. I could not help smiling wryly as I pictured this elegant little item looking entirely out of place in these Spartan surroundings!

Like an excited child, I hugged each item in turn, folding and refolding the tiny clothes, sorting, piling, organizing. What will this wee thing, this product of our love, look like, I mused as I stacked the baby linens into an old dresser drawer in our bedroom.

How will I bathe it, how will I ever keep it warm, I began to worry in earnest. Oh stop, foolish thing, I admonished myself sternly. After all, the baby will not be born until April and surely then it will be much warmer.

Meanwhile, it continues to be bitterly cold, indoors and out. Last Sunday, desperate for a change of scene, Gerard and I ventured to church as usual. We had barely left the shelter of the house for the open field when I became so solidly stuck in a huge snowdrift that I feared momentarily that I might be stranded there permanently. As I wallowed uselessly in the waist deep drift, Gerard tried to dig around me and pull me out. The snow was deathly cold as it crept into my boots and up my dress.

Finally, with one powerful tug, my hero heaved me free from the snowbank and half walked, half carried me back to the house. I was seated in front of the old stove whose dying fire was hurriedly prodded back to life, my feet planted ungraciously in the oven. As Gerard massaged my cold and numbed legs, I urged him to go to church on his own.

"Go! You still have time to make it to the neighbours. I know you look forward to getting out as much as I do."

"No. If you can't go, then I won't either. I don't want to leave you alone. You are cold and exhausted."

"Go!", I commanded. "I'll be just fine. I promise that I will stay right by the fire while you are away. When you return you can tell me all about it! Now, please go."

Reluctantly he departed, leaving me sitting by the stove sipping a hot cocoa and with my feet still in the oven.

Enough of this sitting around, I thought when my cup was emptied. I had observed that most of our precious heat seemed to be going either up the chimney or up the stairwell. One thing was certain, it was not staying in the kitchen and the time had come to do something about it, I decided, setting cup and saucer on the counter.

With that, I ventured bravely to the 'unheated' part of the house, collecting every ancient, tattered blanket and burlap feedbag that I could find. Armed with a hammer and a varied collection of used nails, I proceeded to hang the blankets around the stairwell, thereby closing it off somewhat and creating a colorful circus-tent atmosphere in the kitchen.

My, what a resourceful person you are, I praised myself liberally as I ruthlessly hammered the large rusty nails into the woodwork. The end result of my handiwork was only a minute temperature increase in the kitchen; however, I felt a sense of satisfaction knowing that I had accomplished at least SOMETHING to show my defiance of winter.

If it wasn't for our food supply from the Fathers, I fear that we would have starved to death by now. We are so housebound because of the snow that my only outings now consist of the occasional ride up and down the lane on the bobsled. I do this not so much for the enjoyment of the ride as for the chance to greet whomever from the College is waiting at the highway for the milk.

Exchanging greetings as well as groceries and vegetable scraps for milk, we plod on home again, Prince to the refuge of his stall and I once more to my kitchen.

Eagerly I unpack the food — the flour, sugar, yeast, custard and eggs that I had ordered. Often the cafeteria chef tucks in a few extras — some left-over ham, a soup bone, or even a chicken, one of our former tenants upstairs.

Our staples are bread, pancakes, soup, potatoes, and vegetables from the root cellar. Our dessert usually consists of custard, and with coffee we are enjoying the last of the carefully rationed Christmas goodies.

I try to do as little laundry as possible these days; it has become such a tedious and impossible chore. The house is so cold that even next to the stove the laundry takes two days to dry. I wash socks, underwear and pillowcases regularly but do the heavier items only when absolutely necessary. My one and only pair of slacks will have to wait until spring to be washed

71

for I cannot bear to be without them for a two-day period! We keep our house clothes separate from our barn clothes and this eases the burden of laundering somewhat.

Bathing is another death-defying ritual that calls for courage and stout-heartedness! Slipping into the tub of hot soapy water in front of the stove is usually executed without too much pain and difficulty. Getting out, on the other hand, is quite another matter!

When the moment to leave the mellow warmth of the tub for the frosty air of the kitchen can no longer be postponed, the bather takes a deep breath, plunges from the tub into the towel and then into clean clothes. This procedure is usually accomplished within forty seconds, the motivator being the ever present danger of severe frostbite!

Even I, with my growing midriff, perform this last part of the bathing ritual swiftly and deftly, if not entirely gracefully!

With reference to that midriff, my clothing is becoming painfully tight and restrictive. However, I will have to make do with loosening a button here, a zipper there, perhaps sewing in a dart or two.

We recently have made an amazing discovery about Canadians: they walk on snow! Whereas we sink to our waist step after tortured step, they stroll effortlessly over the drifts, defiantly crunching the white powder underfoot.

On each foot they wear a strange contraption that looks like a skeleton of a cello. To this skeleton, strands of rawhide are affixed in a criss-cross manner. This webbing, apparently, keeps these "snow shoes' from sinking into the snow.

We'll have to find out more about these marvellous contraptions! Perhaps there are other wonderful ways as well to defy the grasp of winter! There remains so much to learn about these mysterious Canadians who are so unaffectedly at home with the cold and the snow.

Gerard and Jane board the Groote Beer in Rotterdam, joining many of their countrymen, all of them seeking a new life across the ocean.

Jane at the door of the church that changed her and Gerard's fortunes.

Below, this is Gerard and Jane's first "home," the uninhabited farmhouse on the Salesian farm they moved into in 1952.

Jane on the tractor that she disliked riding.

Below, Jane and her sister Gonda. Gonda and her husband Marinus were on their way to a new life in California.

Gonda and Marinus' visit is over too soon; they flag down the train and leave for California.

"Surely spring cannot be much further away!"
The waterline to the barn freezes, and the stock comes to the tub
outside the house, to drink.

*Fie, Antoon,
Jane and Gerard*

*A happy Gerard with the lifeblood of a dairy farm —
healthy calves.*

The valiant Prince

Jane and Ben and Trudy

Gerard and Jane, 1988, in a photo taken by their daughter Yvonne. Below, their farm as it looks today, a successful Holstein operation.

12.

A Son is Born

My entire world has been magically rearranged for I have given birth to a precious baby boy! Things are the same, yet wonderfully different, familiar, yet wonderfully new! My heart is filled with sunny days and my emotions contain a new and different intensity that was not there before.

Our son was born on March 18, a full month early but in good health. Except for waking up with some abdominal cramps, that day had started like most other typical winter days; I busied myself in the cold kitchen and tried to hover over the wood stove all at the same time.

By nine o'clock I was experiencing regular bouts of acute abdominal pain that left me doubled over and gasping for breath. When Gerard came in from the barn he immediately suggested that we call Mrs. Grennan, our village public health nurse. We had been informed about Mrs. Grennan after my hospital stay in October and she had been to visit me once or twice since then.

"Let's not, just yet," I suggested, grasping the back of a nearby chair for support. "The baby is not due for another month, so surely these pains will go away."

It soon became obvious that the pains were not going to subside. A hurried telephone call was made to Mrs. Grennan who promised to come by taxi immediately. Gerard then hastily hitched Prince to the sled and travelled down the lane to meet her.

When Mrs. Grennan entered the kitchen she quickly assessed my condition with a knowing eye and said, "Come, Dear, it's time for you to go. Better get your things together and your coat on. I don't think we'll have much time to spare."

As quickly as I could, I collected a few things and tossed them into a suitcase while Mrs. Grannan stood waiting with my coat and boots. Meanwhile, Gerard latched one of the old kitchen chairs onto the bobsled in an effort to make my trip down the lane a bit more bearable.

Finally we were off, Gerard tensely grasping the reins, I clutching desperately to my precarious perch, Mrs. Grennan positioned beside me to offer both physical and moral support, and Prince plodding dutifully along the bumpy trail. From a distance I must have resembled a rotund Cleopatra being carried on a straw-covered float, progressing slowly down a parade route as if to be hailed by the scores of snow drifts on either side!

Finally, mercifully, I was ushered into the warmth of the waiting taxi where I sank heavily into the seat with relief. The first leg of the journey was over.

"Did you want to go back to Dr. Dumas in Campbellton?", Mrs. Grennan asked. I nodded, grimacing with the wave of pain that was slowly washing over me.

Now came the time for Gerard and I to take leave of each other. In Canada, apparently, fathers and childbirth do not belong together, and Mrs. Grennan had already suggested that it would be best for Gerard to stay home.

"She'll be fine," Mrs. Grennan tried to be hastily reassuring. Gerard stood silently helpless and dejected, his hands fumbling uselessly deep within his pockets. "The hospital will call you as soon as there is news," she spoke again, this time with growing urgency.

"We'd better go," she added to the driver. Gerard, as if on cue, bent down quickly and kissed me, his eyes filled with concern.

"Don't worry, I'll be okay," I managed a weak smile.

Throughout the journey Mrs. Grennan studied me carefully and with a knowing eye. Finally she leaned forward and spoke to the driver in a low voice, "We'd better stop in Dalhousie. I don't think that she'll make it to Campbellton."

At the Saint Joseph's Hospital in Dalhousie I was quickly ushered indoors, leaning heavily on Mrs. Grennan as yet another spasm of pain swept through my body. Exhausted and weak, I was placed upon a narrow gurney and covered with a stiff white sheet.

The tiny inadequate hospital was already filled to capacity; consequently my gurney and I were relegated to the hallway where I waited for the physician to examine me.

It is just as good that it is happening this way, suddenly and without much warning, I thought as I shivered under the inflexible sheet. Now I will not have spent the last weeks of my pregnancy worrying about my poor English, what I will say to the physician, how it will all happen. Soon I will be holding my baby and then we can all go home.

"Good afternoon, Ma'am, I am Doctor Bujold," a cheerful voice resonated through the hallway. I looked up to find an intelligent young face smiling down at me.

"Get some blankets for this lady," he called to one of the nurses who scurried away to do his bidding. To me he continued with a series of technical questions to which I could only shake my head apologetically.

Finally he leaned over me, his antiseptic breath gently fanning my face. "Is this your first child?", he asked, forming the words slowly and deliberately and holding up one finger for emphasis.

I nodded, smiling feebly.

"Good, good!", he remarked cheerfully, patting my hand. "That's all I need to know. Don't worry. Everything will be fine. Soon you'll have that baby in your arms."

I was examined and administered a medication to dull the pain. Still shivering uncontrollably, I huddled under the blankets and kept telling myself that soon this would all be a part of the past.

A short time later I was briskly wheeled into an operating room where a mask was momentarily placed over my nose and mouth. Although I was still awake my senses were somewhat deadened, leaving me with a deeply serene feeling that all would be well.

"Congratulations!," Doctor Bujold's voice boomed against the walls of the room, his cheerfulness unabated. "You have a beautiful baby boy! A boy!", he added with emphasis, searching my face to see if I had understood.

I nodded. I understood that I had just given birth to a son.

Back at my station in the hall, I waited anxiously to hold the baby I had managed to catch only a glimpse of as he was being wrapped and whisked away to the nursery.

"Your baby will be here soon, SOON!", a nurse said, approaching my bed on wheels. "He is just fine, FINE!" Offering me a tray of tea and toast, she continued, "We have called your husband."

I smiled and nodded that I had understood.

When the tiny, tightly-wrapped bundle was finally placed in my arms, I hugged him and almost wept for joy. Carefully I opened the blanket to reveal a minute, red-skinned being, his face screwed up as if with livid rage, his spiky dark hair falling stiffly over his forehead. I kissed his cheeks, his forehead, his fists and curled up toes.

"He is beautiful," the nurse at my side beamed, bobbing her head up and down with enthusiastic exaggeration. I bet he looks just like his father!"

I nodded, thinking, he is precious but not beautiful and he certainly doesn't look like his father! His father is handsome, he is but a scrawny, little tyke! Perhaps, if he is lucky, he will look like his father some day!

"What a beautiful baby!", a by now familiar voice called as Doctor Bujold strode towards my bed. "Again, my congratulations! He is small but healthy and you will both be able to go home in five days." He held up five fingers for added emphasis.

Five days? I thought, my spirits sinking. I want to go home tomorrow, today if possible.

In the evening Gerard arrived, bounding over to my bed, his face beaming.

"I saw him at the nursery. He is just beautiful and so are you!" We held each other for several long moments.

"They want me to stay here five days," I said finally.

"I know. I spoke with the doctor for a few minutes. I think it's a good idea."

"You do? Why? Don't you want us home?"

"Of course I want you home. But the baby is small and they want to keep you both here for a few days. Besides, it is cold at home, remember?"

I nodded reluctantly.

"The doctor also told me that all of the hospital beds are taken. He wants to know if you would mind being put into the operating room until a bed becomes available. He says the halls are not very private and quite drafty. Would you mind?"

"No, then at least I won't have to worry about chatting with a roommate. That will be as good a place as any."

"I've sent telegrams to our families," Gerard said suddenly, beaming once more. "They'll be so pleased to know that we have a son."

My five days in the hospital were spent in my bed on wheels in the operating room, and intermittently in the hall when the operating room was in use. Often I strolled down to the nursery to gaze at my son, to hold him, to nurse him.

Gerard visited as often as he could and on his last visit before our discharge, brought with him clothes for the baby to wear on his trip home.

This little fellow really does belong to us, I thought as I dressed him gingerly. He is coming home with us to stay, relying on us totally for love and care. Our loved ones are now his family, our brothers and sisters his aunts and uncles, our parents his grandparents. Oh God, please help us to do the best we can for this precious little boy of ours!

Just before our departure, Gerard went to the nurses' station to inquire where he was to pay for our hospital stay. We had already been told that the cost would be approximately one hundred dollars and Gerard had brought the precious cash with him that morning.

As the nurse was searching for our file, Doctor Bujold came hurrying down the hall. "Glad to have caught you in time," he said jovially, waving the nurse away. "Now, as for our bill," he paused deliberately, dramatically. "Well..., there will be no charge!", he finished triumphantly. "I have been honoured to deliver this beautiful baby, my first foreign baby!"

As we eyed him incredulously, Gerard with a wad of bills in his hand, the doctor exclaimed, "No, No! Put that money away. There is no fee! But the NEXT time however," he chuckled with a playful gleam in his eye, "we will be charging you. We can't make a habit of offering our services for free!"

We grasped the good doctor's hands and poured out our thanks to him as he hung his head bashfully to one side. "It's nothing," he said quietly. "Look after your little one and don't forget to bring him for his checkups. Good luck to your little family."

With that, he turned briskly on his heels and walked quickly away from us.

We have decided to name our son Ben, after Gerard's father, thereby following the Dutch custom that the first born son is named after his paternal grandfather. I hope that someday little Benny will meet his namesake, a good and decent man.

At home, I found a wonderful surprise waiting for me which Gerard proudly presented: a brand new wringer washing machine.

"It's beautiful!", I exclaimed gleefully, removing the cover and gazing into the shiny enamelled tub. "It must have cost a lot of money. Are you sure we can afford it?"

"I got a good deal," Gerard said enthusiastically. "I went with Brother Gerard to a store where the Fathers always do their business. The owner even sent along a little gift for you." With that, he offered me a box containing a pair of tiny, delicate blue booties.

This is a wonderful world we live in, where even strangers extend their kindness to us. How lucky we are to have been flung by Providence to this far corner of the world that, although cold, isolated and far from wealthy, is filled with caring and charitable people.

13.

A Vigil of Hope
and Heartbreak

The month of April started out with so much promise; who could have foretold that a long, enduring nightmare was about to be unfolded. Early in the month we had our first spring thaw. Although it did little to loosen the grip of winter, it was a glorious day to behold and did wonders for the winter-weary spirit. The sun shone brilliantly, melting snow on the roof and sending tiny rivulets of water gurgling along the eaves of the house. Even a few hardy birds had been cajoled by Mother Nature to sing exuberantly from their perch on the telephone wire.

With a song of my own in my heart, I tended to the needs of my new son who, although still so tiny, seemed to be growing, albeit at a modest pace.

"Just wait until summer comes, My Little One," I spoke softly to the bundle in my arms as we waltzed around the kitchen table. "We'll put your bonnet on and take you for long walks in the sunshine. THEN we'll see a little boy begin to thrive!"

Mere days later I began to experience a hot, stinging sensation in my breasts. I chose to ignore the discomfort, reassuring myself that mother and child were, after all, still new at this feeding business and that some tenderness was to be expected. When the pain became increasingly difficult to ignore, and when my breasts became hard and impliable, I began to worry that our son was not getting enough nourishment. Finally, when my nipples began to expell a thick, purulent, greyish liquid, and the baby could no longer nurse, I knew the time had come to return to Doctor Bujold.

At his office, Doctor Bujold examined little Benny swiftly and intently.

"Your little fellow is starving," he told us tersely but not unkindly. "And now I want to see you, Jane," he motioned to me as he handed our son to Gerard.

Under his scrutinizing eyes I lay timidly, daring only to stare at the blank ceiling as the searing heat emanated from my exposed breasts. Finally Doctor Bujold spoke.

"Is there T.B. in your family?"

I turned my head to look at him blankly, not comprehending the question.

"T.B.," he repeated patiently but with growing urgency. "Has anyone in your family ever had tuberculosis?" He enunciated at what for him must have been a painfully slow pace.

Tuberculosis, I mulled over the word. Oh. . . . tuberculOSE, I suddenly comprehended as the dreaded significance of the question rapidly washed over me. My mother had lost several siblings to tuberculosis. During the war years, thousands of Dutch people had succumbed to tuberculosis, the most feared disease of that time.

"Yes," I managed to whisper in reply, although Doctor Bujold has already seen the answer in my frightened eyes.

"I'm sorry to frighten you this way," he soothed, taking my hand in his. "But I want you to go to the hospital immediately for x-rays and tests. We'll talk when the tests have been completed."

In a state of shock, we trudged heavily through the packed and soiled snow to the hospital nearby, Gerard with Benny in one arm and his other held tightly around my shoulder.

"T.B.", I kept whispering as my eyes filled with unwelcome tears.

"Maybe, only MAYBE," Gerard emphasized sternly,

hugging me closer to his side. "Let's wait until the tests are done before we begin to worry," his words sounded like a command intended as much for himself as it was for me.

Swiftly the tests were conducted and soon Doctor Bujold and Gerard were again at my side.

"We still don't know," Doctor Bujold began. "You'll have to stay here for a few days while we do a biopsy. A biopsy," he repeated slowly. "It is only minor surgery and will tell us for certain what the problem is."

"But the baby — ," I began a futile protest.

"The baby will stay too. Our nursery is full but we will find room for him somewhere. He's undernourished and needs some tending to as well."

Nodding feebly, we could only agree with these arrangements.

When the biopsy results had come back negative a few days later, I allowed some of my worries to subside. The cursed tuberculosis had not travelled across the Atlantic with me after all. Just a very bad case of mastitis, I had been assured.

My thoughts now changed to my son whom I had not seen for a few days. Eager to hold the child once again, I sought out Doctor Bujold while on his rounds.

"I want to see my baby," I demanded as emphatically as I could. He seemed strangely troubled by my request but suggested only that I no longer try to breastfeed him.

Anxious to be reunited with my beloved child, I hurried down to the nursery and sought out his little face among the row of bassinets arranged behind the large window. The child I was looking for was not there. Apprehensively I approached a nurse who was tending a newborn and asked to see my son. Wordlessly but with sadness in her eyes, she patted my shoulder briefly and motioned to a lone bassinet in the far corner of the nursery.

Something must be wrong, I thought, suddenly panic-stricken as I tiptoed over to the crib. I dared to peer among the little bed linens and was horrified by what I saw. This can't be my child, I cried inwardly, as I observed the pinched little face, the hollow cheeks, the blue, almost waxy, translucent pallor. This was a child who hovered near death, its tiny frail body curled tightly inward on itself. Certainly this could NOT be my baby. I studied his sleeping face closely in the way that one observes a stranger's child. In that sick little child I saw nothing that I recognized.

"That is not my baby," I insisted to the nurse, my eyes pleading with her to tell me that she had simply made a mistake. She shook her head slowly, sadly, her shoulders sagging suddenly.

"I'm sorry," she finally spoke quietly, much too quietly. "He is very sick. I can't tell you anything. You must speak with the doctor." Briefly she held my hollow stare, then turned her attention to the robust infant on the table, her efficient hands deftly manoeuvering the child into a clean nightshirt.

Back in my room, I crouched on the bed and wept softly, my fists thrust into my hot, stinging eyes. "Why, God, why?", my tortured soul cried out into the emptiness. We were doing so well, our little threesome. We had almost survived the winter. We were beginning to adjust to our new surroundings. Above all, we had parented a child, a Canadian child who should have been destined to inherit a whole new way of life. Now, it seemed, this child was going to die, its brief life a stark testimony to the rugged frontier life that we had subjected it to.

The firm hand that was gently placed on my shoulder belonged to Doctor Bujold who had wordlessly made his way over to my bed. Perching himself on its edge, he waited quietly until I raised my head to peer at him over my tear-streaked arm.

"Mrs. Duivenvoorden, I'm very sorry," he began in a soft voice, the characteristic cheerful loudness notably absent. "The nurse should not have said anything to you. I was going to tell you and your husband today, now that your own worries are over, that yes, your baby is very sick."

Shaking his head he continued, "When you arrived we really had no room for him so we placed him in a bassinet with a newborn. When we realized a day or two later that the other child had pneumonia, we separated the infants immediately. However, Benny soon began showing the symptoms of pneumonia."

He sighed heavily as he rearranged himself on the edge of the bed. "He has a very severe case of diarrhea which is serious in babies as tiny as he is. If we can manage to stop the diarrhea and have him gain some weight, he will have a chance."

After a lengthy pause, he added, "I will look after him, Jane, as if he were my own."

"Gerard is coming today," was all I could manage in response.

Later that afternoon, Gerard and I huddled wordlessly over the tiny bassinet that held the child neither of us recognized to be our own. We listened to the laboured puffs of breath and watched in shock as the tiny heaving chest and gaping mouth struggled in unison to keep this miniature being alive. Stunned, we finally returned to my room where we held each other for a long time.

When Doctor Bujold joined us, he repeated what he had told me earlier, emphasizing that Benny would receive his utmost care and attention.

That night, in the quiet emptiness of my hospital room, I knelt on the bed and prayed for my son's survival. No, pleaded is a better word, I pleaded with God to give this child a chance to experience the life that we had chosen for him. I begged Him not to take away the precious gift of parenthood that had so recently been bestowed upon us.

Finally, exhausted, I climbed under the covers and prayed for my dear Gerard who must also have been grappling with his emotions in our lonely, empty, comfortless house.

After a week of hospitalization, I was allowed to return home. I was still sore and tender but refused to acknowledge the pain, preparing instead to struggle with the hour when I must take leave of my child.

"He will receive the best of our care," Doctor Bujold tried to be reassuring. "You may call me every night at home, and I will tell you how he is doing. Every day that he survives is a day gained. He is a fighter, so he has a chance."

And so our days had evolved around our evening telephone calls to the good Doctor. Always, we hasten to ask how the baby is. And always, the response is cautious, reserved.

"He still has diarrhea. If we can only stop the diarrhea, he'll be okay."

"He is getting better but he still has diarrhea."

"He has gained two ounces today."

Finally, we dared to ask if we could come to see him, to take him home.

"Oh, no, that would be impossible. He is still much too small to go home. It is better that you don't come at all until he has gained more weight."

While I was still in hospital, Gerard had prepared a telegram to send overseas. The thought of worrying our dear ones so far away with such grave news troubled us and made us hesitant to send it. "Let's not," we suggested to each other after a lengthy discussion. We reasoned that once the child had recovered, as we stubbornly ascertained that it would, we would send a letter recounting our trials and illnesses. If, on the other hand, the unthinkable happened, we would be able to dispatch the news via telegram swiftly enough.

The vigil continues, slowly, painfully. The hollow, lifeless ticking of the kitchen clock inches away the minutes, hours, half-days. Every evening we gather breathlessly around the telephone, its tattered cord our fragile lifeline to our beloved son. Every evening, as the shadow of darkness falls around us and the telephone is again gingerly placed in its cradle, we vehemently reassure ourselves that he is still alive and that we must not lose hope. And every evening we fall asleep with our prayers echoing in our ears that this enduring trial will soon be part of the faceless, timeless past.

14.

A Triumphant Homecoming

On this last day in May, this glorious Sunday afternoon, there is much to rejoice. Our baby has come home to his family! After what seemed like an endless number of evening telephone calls to Doctor Bujold, the longed-for words were finally spoken: our baby was ready to leave the hospital. In the same breath Doctor Bujold cautioned us, however, that we would find him still very thin and tiny, not at all like the child we had originally left behind in the nursery.

Indeed, we were shocked by his emaciated state but remained undaunted about the prospect of taking him home. I was actually relieved to be delivering him from the hospital and into my own care where he would surely benefit from my undivided attention.

I tried to listen attentively to the list of instructions that was being recited by the nurse, much as a child concentrates unsuccessfully on a tedious sermon that he knows will be followed by the distribution of wonderful gifts. I was to feed the baby every two hours, day and night and return for a checkup in one week's time.

Finally we three were dismissed, Gerard was handed a case of baby formula, and our elated little family was allowed to descend the hospital steps. It was May 18 and the tight green buds on the trees seemed to burst forth with new growth and vigor. Even the ordinary little sparrows on the telephone wire chirped in exuberant unison, their chorus-line song seeming to welcome us home in glorious triumph.

After a week of twelve feedings per day, we again appeared before Doctor Bujold who readily proclaimed his satisfaction with Benny's progress. "Very good , hmmm . . . VERY good," he muttered to himself as he gently examined the fledgling infant.

"Well done," he addressed us encouragingly when the examination was complete. "He is already doing much better, even beginning to grow a little. From now on he will require only two night feedings."

Although I would have gladly fed and cared for him every minute of the day and night, had this continued to be necessary, the instruction to reduce night feedings was music to my ears. The relief must have been written in my eyes for Doctor Bujold added quietly, "And you must get some rest too, Jane. You look exhausted."

In the past week we have been joined by Gerard's younger brother, Antoon, and his young wife, Fie — short for Sophia. He is a well-built man of average height, eager to explore his new surroundings and ready to act on any opportunity that is presented. (Both Gerard and Antoon spent a number of years with the Dutch military in Indonesia; perhaps it is this jungle experience that has given them a thrist for new challenges and a general fascination for unknown frontiers. How else would they/we ever have ended up here, in this isolated little corner of the world!)

Fie, who is expecting their first child in November, is a tall blond girl from one of the neighbouring villages in Holland. Although I do not know her well, it is wonderful to have them here and prattle away in our beloved Dutch language. They have come bearing letters, parcels, and precious news from Home, and I have blatantly relished all of it.

We had known of their impendent arrival for some time and Gerard had already finalized arrangements with the Fathers for Antoon to work on this farm for six months. They will be living with us at least until the fall, at which time they hope to strike out on their own.

After a long winter's sojourn, we have resumed our English lessons with Father Mario. Father says that we have actually improved noticeably, an improvement more than likely prompted by our recent difficulties. In truth, one's shyness to speak is shed very quickly when the welfare of one's loved ones is at stake. Hence, even I am now finding it less difficult to summon my English vocabulary to my tongue!

Our precious savings account at the local bank has been totally depleted, following payment of the hospital bill for myself and little Benny's care. Although Doctor Bujold refused to accept payment for his personal services (I suspect he feels very badly that Benny was originally bedded with a sick infant), the hospital costs nonetheless added up to a staggering seven hundred dollars. We have paid that amount ungrudgingly, however, feeling only gratitude that this family crisis is solidly behind us.

So, financially, we are starting from zero once again. But we remain optimistic that it will be a good summer, with better crops and therefore better harvests, a bountious vegetable garden, the continued kindness of the Fathers, and Antoon helping with the farm work. Most of all, we have our love and our health; has humankind really ever needed more than that?

15.

The Geography Lesson

Incredibly, today marks the first anniversary of our arrival in Canada! As I sit mending at my sunny kitchen table, a large vase of fresh, fragrant lilacs in front of me, a sleeping infant in the carriage at my side, I have great difficulty recollecting what we must have been experiencing one mere short year ago.

Like two souls who had long been adrift in the vast sea of the unknown, we had gingerly set foot on Canadian soil in Halifax and had tottered uncertainly around the dismally drab harbourfront. In the Colonist Train, as we now know this train was called, it being a train used only for the transportation of immigrants, we had huddled together grimly, silently, swaying mechanically to the wearisome but yet hypnotic rhythm of steel wheels on steel rails.

Even now, to dwell on our journey and our first month's ordeal is to automatically usher an icy finger of frigid cold to every bone in my body. I suspect that the memories of this arduous period and the chilling effect incited by their recollection will remain with me forever.

Who could have known that such a precarious start coud have so quickly culminated in this, our "own" farm, a precious child, and even a pair of relatives to share our lives? Who could have known that, after the hostile and inhospitable

Black family, there would be the wonderfully kindhearted Fathers, those charitable Men of God whose help is offered in such a way that one's dignity and pride are not affected nor marred? Who indeed, could have known that we would find our new Canadian neighbours, still strangers in so many ways, to be accepting of our presence in their midst?

Yes, Canada does seem to have been the right choice for us. Although we have no great personal wealth, we are able to exercise wonderful freedoms: an abundance of territory to explore (unlike Holland, there seems to be no great notion of private property here, therefore a "stroll" can literally lead to anywhere), and more arable land than the area farmers can manage. True, the quality of the land, with its general unevenness and endless cache of rocks and bramble, is considerably less than the farmland of Holland, but it is the POTENTIAL here that is so unlimited.

And still . . . I do so sorely miss the friendly, noisy crowdedness of the Dutch villages, the unruly banterings of the colorful marketplace, the orderly postage stamp-sized lawns and gardens with their manicured rows of spring tulips. I miss the majestic windmills that dot and dominate the endlessly flat horizon, their sails slicing gracefully and perpetually through the air. But mostly, I miss my family, so often my heart aches longingly for them. I dream of introducing my son to his grandparents, to the gaggle of aunts and uncles who would surely dote over him with a rare indulgence reserved only for the children of long lost relatives! I long for the aroma of real Dutch coffee, for the clatter of coffee cups, and the endless, sometimes aimless, chatter of young and old alike.

Yet, Canada is where we really belong now, I must keep reminding myself of this, must never allow myself to sway from this conviction. Gerard seems truly happy here; he knows that his hard work will lead to almost endless opportunities for his family. Already I suspect that he genuinely loves this place and is filled with the vision of what this farm could become. And now, with Antoon working by his side, he seems even more serene and content with our lot in life.

We celebrated our first wedding anniversary on June 17 and proclaimed the day to be somewhat of a holiday. While

Gerard and Antoon tended to the essential chores, Fie and I cleaned up the kitchen, bathed little Benny, and picked a generous bouquet of the lilacs that are growing so profusely in our front garden. We celebrated with a walk to the beach, several games of cards, and endless cups of coffee garnished with a package of store-bought cookies. (Oh, but to sink my teeth into a glorious Dutch cream puff pastry just one more time!)

On this day Gerard also produced a tattered map which, he teasingly explained as he unfolded it elaborately, was for "Sjaan to get an idea of where we are!" Eagerly we all crowded around the table as Gerard pinpointed our present location and traced a line from it across the vast Atlantic, coming to a halt at our former little Homeland.

"And this," Gerard swept his left hand over the map in dramatic fashion, "This is all of Canada!"

"All of that is Canada?", we breathed incredulously, not believing that any one country could be so large.

"You could actually live in some parts of Western Canada and be farther away from us than the people of Holland are!" Gerard continued triumphantly. He had always had a propensity for geography and was thoroughly revelling in this little teaching session.

Even Antoon was left wordless as he attempted to digest the significance of the vast dimensions of Canada. Or perhaps he was simply dumfounded by dancing visions of the endless possible Canadian destinations from which to choose a home for himself and his unsuspecting bride.

Looking up from my mending for a brief moment, my eyes gaze across the kitchen and through the east window, coming to rest on a small homely shack on the other side of the pasture. Its occupants, the Henssons, seem to have some puzzling peculiarities about them. For one thing, how they managed to survive the winter in that inadequate, weather-ravaged shack is totally beyond my imagination.

Joe, the head of the family, claims to be of Nordic descent and seems to be one of the few literate people in the community. His constant companion is a brown, long-necked bottle tucked into a tattered breast pocket. "Want a drink,

Janey?", he never fails to ask when we chance to meet. I always wordlessly shake my head in response.

Hensson's wife is a stern-faced woman who rarely leaves the shack and is therefore scarcely seen at all. They have several children including a teenage daughter, Maria, who appears to have offspring of her own. A number of times during the past winter, Joe and one or two sons have presented themselves on our doorstep with an empty baby bottle, asking for "milk for the baby," presumably Maria's youngest.

As I washed the soured, encrusted residue from the dirty bottle's rim and filled it with fresh milk, I could not help but worry about the fate of a hungry baby in such cold, sparse surroundings. My worries were not quelled, when, observing their slow plodding journey back to the shack, I noticed the baby bottle being passed from one to another, each in turn stopping long enough to throw back his head and take a long thirsty draft. Grimly I wondered if any of the milk would find its way to the hungry child's lips.

In early spring one of the Hensson boys, Jake, started to come around, at first infrequently but then on a fairly regular basis. His curiosity with us was unbridled, often his mouth hung slightly agape as he listened to our quick exchanges in Dutch. When we addressed him he would respond with a silly grin and a loud, uncomprehending laugh.

Eventually, he began to follow Gerard around and attempted to help with some of the simple chores.

"Poor fellow," Gerard would say, shaking his head sympathetically. "I think he's had a miserable home life."

Although Jake roamed around the yard quite freely for a time, I had no fear of him and considered him to be quite harmless. Gerard tolerated his new found shadow good-naturedly and began to devise simple tasks for him to do so that we could offer him food and the occasional handful of tobacco "in return." He is always grateful for these offerings, reacting in the way of a child who has unexpectedly been given a dime to spend in a candy store.

He is about twenty-four years of age and wears a shock of thick dark hair over large brown eyes that look as if he's perpetually trying to understand his complex surroundings.

He seems to be rather dull mentally, and has never had any formal education. Still, he is a cheerful sort of fellow and eager to please in his own way. At the moment he is away and our neighbours tell us that we will not see him again until fall. Apparently he spends the summers roaming from one village to another.

One wonders what is to become of such a fellow. Plainly, his family is of little consolation and support to him. With his limited talent and potential, will he ever find a niche for himself? Will we ever see him again?

16.

Kitchen Curtains and Birthday Cake

The houseflies are back in driving force! I've resorted once more to placing inverted bowls over all exposed food, and the baby carriage is carefully draped with mosquito netting even in, no, ESPECIALLY in the kitchen! The twin fly swatters are constantly in use and every few days the sticky fly papers that hang from the ceiling like sodden, blackened party streamers, so laden with clinging insect corpses are they, are replaced with fresh ones. And yet, for all our efforts, their numbers never seem to diminish; indeed, I suspect that they are thriving as they buzz loudly on the window sills and walk boldly across the kitchen table!

I think Fie finds all these flies overwhelming, much as I did last year at this time. She waves her arms at them irritably and, armed with one of the fly swatters, stalks them with a vengeance!

"There! THAT one is dead!", she declares triumphantly one hundred times a day.

From my point of view, the flies are not nearly the concern that our rodent problem is. The house is literally overrun with mice, their brazen activity being carried on as much in the day as in the still of the night. I was nearly startled out of my wits last week when, reaching for a box of cookies in a drawer, out jumped a fat ugly mouse who had obviously been dining there for some time.

"We've got to do something," I insisted to Gerard. "The mice are driving me crazy! And I can't stand their little black litterings all over the place either!"

Consequently, we've recruited a couple of lean felines from the barn, who, after regarding their new environment with some apprehension, have happily settled into their appointed role. I know their presence is having an effect on the rodent population; the scurrying sounds within the walls have been noticeably reduced, and occasionally one of the proud mousers will present a bloodied, battered rodent remnant at my feet. Needless to say, the offering does little to thrill me but I never fail to shower the cat with lavish praise. I will not rest easy until every last mouse has been banished from the house.

We have acquired a new luxury in the kitchen: a refrigerator purchased by Antoon and Fie. I suspect that Antoon has had his fill of tinned meats and since our cellar is not cold enough in summer to store fresh meat and other perishables on a prolonged basis, we have up until now been eating much of our food out of tins.

Now we can enjoy ice-cold milk or lemonade, fresh produce (when the local store has it in stock, which is not often), and fresh meat. No longer need we worry about the butter going rancid and the mayonnaise spoiling.

Our beautiful baby has regained his health and is growing steadily. Every day his bright little smile and alert eyes fill me with overwhelming gratitude that God saw fit to spare him and leave him in our care.

On the advice of the Fathers, we have taken out an insurance policy specifically for hospital and medical expenses. Gerard seems satisfied that this monthly expense is well worth the peace of mind that the insurance will offer us. We would never want to find ourselves in the agonizing position of not being financially able to seek the best health care available for our family.

Our bank account is very slowly being replenished; however, it will be some time before the seven hundred dollars that we had managed to save will be regained. I harbour no regrets through, being only grateful that the money was there when we needed it.

And still, a part of me is convinced that, had we genuinely not been capable of paying our medical expenses, some alternative arrangements for payment would have been made by the hospital. After all, not once were we asked if we would be able to pay for Benny's care; no one seemed too concerned about the financial aspects of our son's illness. It seems to be the Canadian way "not to worry about it, we'll work something out later." Certainly the Canadian society that we have been exposed to is not nearly as financially oriented as are the Dutch people. It seems that here money is not nearly as important in the day-to-day lives of the people.

Fie and I find many tasks to fill each day. Aside from the baby's care (which I jealously guard as my own exclusive territory!) and the challenges associated with keeping this roughly hewn house clean and its tenants fed, we have been indulging in a bit of basic redecorating.

On a recent rare trip to town Fie and I, with visions of cheery kitchen curtains fluttering gracefully in our minds, selected a few metres of colourfully striped cotton. We came home feeling pleased that we had paid so little for the fabric, that we had gotten such a good 'deal." Our pleasure soon waned however when, upon washing the cotton, we found, to our dismay, that it had shrunk and tattered terribly.

"How can they sell such cheap stuff?", we inquired of each other as we nonetheless attempted to sew the pathetic fabric into little curtains. "In Holland, they would never sell material so poor in quality! No wonder we paid so little for it! It's not even worth what we paid!"

And so we consoled ourselves as we arranged the pitiful little things in the windows, the limp, lifeless fabric already faded after one careful washing.

It is true that in Holland such goods would not be offered for sale. The Dutch generally pride themselves in their workmanship, be it in the manufacture of clothing, china, or of ordinary farm tools. Here, it seems that one has to be very selective when making a purchase, recognizing that sub-standard merchandise is seemingly displayed next to the quality items without explanation, apology, or hint of embarrassment.   Apparently, the difference in price is explanation enough!

However, our faded little curtains do flutter in the summer breeze after all, and also serve to hide the hordes of flies that hover noisily around the sills. And next time, I won't be caught quite so unaware when making a household purchase!

Fie and I have also been tending the many little seedlings in the garden. Already we are enjoying the tender little lettuce greens and wait impatiently for the slender, succulent beans that will follow in a few weeks.

Today is Gerard's twenty-eighth birthday, an occasion that called for a cake (Yes, I've been practising my baking again, this time with limited success!). Other than that, it's been a normal Sunday, with our usual unhurried stroll, this time through the woods behind the railway tracks.

Gerard is a wonderful man, kind and caring, strong and always calm. Coming to Canada was a definite disquietude for me; coming with Gerard somehow made the adventure just a bit easier and less unrealistic. When first contemplating our emigration from Holland, Gerard must have known that I would follow him anywhere, albeit with reluctance! Suffice it to say that a Dutch country girl like myself would have never ended up here on her own!

17.

A Date with the Dentist

The month of August has offered us some real insights into community life in this area. It seems that the more we attempt to branch out and expand our narrow horizons, the more we find that there is much to learn about the community into which we have been so haply relocated.

The people we have met here are so different from the Black family; their simple, unpretentious ways and their acceptance of us are making our transition from foreigners to neighbours immeasurably less difficult than it would be under dissimilar circumstances. Had we stayed with the Black family longer, we would have gained a horribly distorted impression of the Canadian people, a negativism about Canada that in all probability would have lingered within us for years.

The little neighbourhood store is a befitting example of the basic kindness and goodness that seems inherent in so many of the people here. For some time now we have been supplementing the groceries brought by the Fathers with goods purchased at our neighbourhood store. Fie and I always enjoy the unhurried mid-afternoon stroll to and from the store, pushing the carriage and discussing our purchases at great length.

Once at the store, our incessant chatter is quickly reduced to shy smiles and vigorous nods as we timidly point to the items we want to purchase. Not being able to read English however, we have more than once selected an unfamiliar package, the contents of which have been a real surprise!

The store occupies the living room of the home of a middle-aged couple whom we know as Delphis and Mrs. Delphis. (I suspect that Delphis is the man's first name; however, the lady does not seem to mind being addressed as Mrs. Delphis.) Both Delphis and Mrs. Delphis, whoever is minding the store on any given day, wait patiently behind the spotless counter while Fie and I roam timidly around the premises and study the unfamiliar goods that line the homemade shelves. When our selections have finally been made, the items are carefully packed in a brown paper bag and the bill is totalled.

Now I must confess that the Canadian currency and coinage is still very foreign to me and I become hopelessly confused whenever I attempt to count out any particular amount of money. Consequently, I smile apologetically and with a blush of embarrassment, and hold out a handful of small bills and various coins for the proprietor to count. This is always done obligingly and the change is always gently placed in my waiting hand.

It would be so easy for these people to take advantage of us, and yet I fervently believe that they never do. As with most of the other neighbours we have met to date, the Delphises seem to be goodhearted people to whom money matters little in life.

"Thank you, Dear!", Mrs. Delphis always says warmly, handing me the bulging paper bag. "And how is that little fellow of yours today?" Turing to Fie, she will add in a concerned voice, "And how are you feeling today, Dear?"

We are finding that groceries cost much less here than they did back Home. Items such as sugar, flour, and shortening seem to cost only a fraction of what their Dutch price tag would be. Perhaps, now that the War and Occupation are over and food staples are once again widely available Overseas, prices there have also been reduced to within reason.

In any event, I am finding that it really doesn't cost that much to feed a family in this part of Canada. Groceries are not expensive, the garden is an oasis of tender vegetables, our supply of fresh milk is virtually unlimited, and our good friends, the Fathers, keep bringing us little surprise packages from their cafeteria. It is clear that we have nothing to complain about!

We have also gotten to know Mrs. Olive who operates a tiny Post Office out of her back porch, just a few houses away from Mrs. Delphis' store. (Her name in fact is Olive Lawlor but we've quite naturally fallen into the habit of calling her 'Mrs. Olive.') Everything about her appearance suggests a kind, motherly character who is never at a loss for cheerful, encouraging words.

"Oh look!", she will often exclaim enthusiastically, her fine facial lines stretching into an enormous smile, "A letter from Home! How exciting for you!" Observing her obvious pleasure as she produces the latest blue airmail envelope, one would be inclined to think that she had been anticipating this most recent news from Home as much as we!

As of late, I've begun to 'socialize' a bit with a few of the neighbouring women. No, no, I haven't been the one to initiate this for I remain the eternal faintheart when it comes to conversing in English! Rather, some of the women have started to visit on occasion, at first to see the baby and more lately to pay us social calls.

We've started to play cards (I would venture to say that ninety-five percent of the Dutch population are fervent card players, we being no exception!) with two of our immediate neighbours, Imelda and Christine. They are a goodnatured pair who have taken it upon themselves to teach us 'Auction 45.' Apparently the games with which we are familiar, 'Klaverjassen' and 'Hartenjagen' are not known here.

They are enthusiastic players, laughing jovially as cards are exuberantly slapped upon the table. Any void in the chatter that is due to our lack of conversation is quickly and easily filled with their cheerful banter. Actually, I am secretly pleased with how much of their conversation I am able to understand, although I venture to say little. Antoon and Fie, I know, understand very little and Gerard, on the other hand, probably understands most of what they say.

Still, as unlikely a group we are, there is always an ample supply of good cheer on hand and endless cups of coffee for us, tea for the guests. Tea does seem to be the preferred drink here; in Holland, tea is often served with breakfast and then the teapot is retired to the shelf until the following morning! The Dutch are a nation of avid coffee lovers!

During one of our recent card games, the topic turned to hairstyles, probably as a result of my most recent attempt to trim my own thick mass of unruly tresses. Prior to leaving Holland I had subjected my straight hair to a permanent wave. Now, fourteen months and several self-inflicted haircuts later, my hairstyle had essentially been reduced to a mop of straight dark hair punctuated with the occasional tenacious, uncooperative remnant of a curl.

"You know Jane, Margie does a real good job with a perm, doesn't she Melda?", this from Christine as the cards were being dealt yet again, Imelda nodding in agreement. Margie is the woman whose children struggled up our lane with a gift of home baking on Christmas day. We see her in church frequently and always exchange friendly smiles of recognition.

"And Margie would come to the house, bring all her stuff, set you on a chair and just do it."

"You wouldn't have to leave the house, she'd just come here, she's good, and she doesn't cost much."

"She does everybody's hair around here, does a good job too! We'll let her know you want your hair done!"

I nodded in agreement, eyeing the tightly coiffed curls of our two guests who had meanwhile refocused their attention to the hand being played. I would give Margie a try, being in dire need of a good cut and other drastic measures to regain control of the crop on top of my head.

True to their word, the ladies contacted Margie who presented herself on my doorstep a few days later. Briskly and deftly she combed and clipped and curled and styled, her slow calm voice keeping up a steady, mostly one-sided conversation.

"There!", she nodded with satisfaction, leading me to

the nearest mirror where I prepared to greet the new me with some apprehension. Actually I was pleasantly surprised by the near shoulder-length collection of orderly curls that adorned my head.

"Not bad!", Fie commented after Margie had left. For the last few days the chemical fumes have steadily emanated from my hair, causing Fie and her fragile stomach to keep their distance. Each time he enters the house, Gerard sniffs the air with exaggerated question and shakes his head teasingly. His own "army cut" is easy enough to keep trimmed; he bemusedly regards my new hairdo as something totally alien and incomprehensible to all men.

Another first this month was a trip to the dentist for Gerard who reluctantly accompanied the Fathers on one of their outings to town. Before his departure, he consulted the Dutch-English "woordenboek" for the English version of the word, "appointment."

"Got it!", he exclaimed triumphantly, slapping the book shut. "And now, once and for all, I'll get this miserable tooth fixed!" A molar in need of repair had been bothering him for some time.

A few hours later, a still red-faced Gerard came home, hanging his head and smiling sheepishly.

"How did it go?", I asked anxiously. "Did you get an appointment? Did you get your tooth fixed?"

"That dictionary of ours is no good!", he grinned wearily with just a hint of a chuckle in his voice. "Come sit and I'll tell you all about my adventure."

It seems that Gerard had entered the dentist's office in a confident mood, marched up to the young receptionist seated behind a large desk, and stated loudly, "I would like to make a date!"

"P-Pardon?", the young woman flustered, a slight blush beginning to creep over her cheeks.

"I want to make a date. I want a date!", Gerard repeated determinedly. He had come all this way for an appointment and was not prepared to leave without one.

"But you can't, I'm sorry!", the lady stammered,

gulping deeply and shaking her head vigorously, her eyes cast low upon the paperwork in front of her.

"Why not?", Gerard demanded to know, the anger slowly rising within his chest.

"Because I'm married," she replied in a tiny, pleading voice.

"I don't CARE if you're married! I want a date! NOW!", Gerard raised his voice out of frustration and impatience. It was clear to him that the woman didn't know what he was talking about, nor did he know why she seemed so ill at ease.

A moment of uncomfortable silence ticked slowly by. Then suddenly the woman flashed angry eyes at Gerard and snapped at him with new-found courage, "Exactly what is it that you want?"

"Look!", Gerard said, his own patience also beginning to wear thin. He took a decisive step toward the desk and opened his mouth to display the cause of the confusion. "I need a date to have my tooth fixed! Can you see it there?" He tugged his cheek away from the orderly row of white molars that lined his lower jaw.

A wave of relief washed over the woman and she instantaneously broke into a clear, brilliant smile of relief. "You want an APPOINTMENT!", she bubbled enthusiastically, barely able to contain her sudden amusement. "You want an APPOINTMENT to have your tooth fixed! Let me make an APPOINTMENT for you." She took great pleasure in repeatedly emphasizing the word that had magically dissolved an awkward situation.

As she scribbled something on a small card, she swallowed and asked softly, "Do you know what the word 'date' actually means?" It was Gerard's turn to blush with embarrassment.

Now, blushing again at the recollection of the episode, Gerard shook his head and said to me resignedly, "This English business, it's pretty tough. And that book," he shook his fist at the dictionary in mock fury, "that book almost got me into a lot of trouble!"

"Next time, I think I'll consult with the Fathers first," Gerard nodded as he mentally concluded the entire distasteful episode, his face taking on a martyred expression that prompted us both to dissolve into light-headed laughter.

The summer is passing much too quickly. How I enjoy the sounds of the plump yellow honey bees as they buzz unaffectedly amongst the nodding purple heads of clover in the yard, and of the dry crunch of the gritty gravel underfoot in the driveway. How I savor the pure redolent perfume of the wild roses that grow in a tangled mass along the side of the house. And how I indulge with unrestrained, even paganistic delight in the sweet succulence of crisp young lettuce and tender green beans.

These are the sights, sounds and smells and tastes that I will commend to my memory, to be called upon and lingered over on a cold January day when the splendor and compassion of summer seem light years away.

18.

Saints in the Attic

Our second Canadian summer has come and gone; already the nights are cool and a new freshness and crispness lingers in the early morning air. Gone is the sweltering afternoon sun that brought generous beads of sweat to the dust-covered foreheads of the toilers in the hay fields. Even the houseflies have toned down the vigor of their activities in preparation for hibernation or whatever it is that flies do to survive the winter.

Armed with a palette of rich ocher, Mother Nature is preparing to embellish the landscape with one last extravagant brush stroke before covering it entirely and completely in pristine white. The summer flowers are beginning to droop forlornly, their delicate frost-tinged heads sadly shrunken like sodden tissue paper.

Much of the summer's harvest has been completed; the hay, grain, and potato crops are noticeably improved over last year's meagre bounty. When time allows, Gerard and Antoon continue to haul firewood from the bush which is then sawed into manageable lengths by a screaming, ugly-toothed steel blade powered by the tractor. Fie and I stack the freshly cut wood into orderly rows, breathing in the pure, balmy perfume of the wood sap as it mingles with the invigoratingly cool air.

The tasks of autumn and the many preparations for winter are good for the heart as well as the soul. The work is healthy and enjoyable: the satisfaction derived from readying shelter and fuel and food supplies against the coming onslaughts of nature stirs up deep feelings of inner serenity and peace of mind.

With all of our domestic doings, we have still managed, unwittingly, to become embroiled in yet another confusing adventure in our newly adopted language! We are no longer taking lessons from Father Mario who announced some time ago that in future, practise would be our most effective teacher. Gerard still has difficulty with his "th's" and "sh's," enunciating at times with obviously uncontrolled abandon. At other times a "th" sound will suddenly appear in his speech where none belongs, or it will be noticeably and flatly absent in the words that require the whispery addition for proper elocution.

Our most recent misadventure took place within the revered walls of the church, as we proceeded to settle ourselves in for yet another Sunday morning service. As usual, Gerard quietly and unobtrusively escorted me, with Benny in my arms, to our usual pew near the front of the church. We found it occupied by a burly but congenial looking fellow named Pauly, who had installed himself on the aisle end of the seat. The surrounding pews were filled and the service was about to begin.

"Excuse me," Gerard began in a loud whisper, his English at its careful best. "Could we," he motioned to include me and the child, "Could we shh-it here please?"

An instant and unrestrained smile broke out on Pauly's face as he slid over to make room for us. Behind him and across the aisle, hushed giggles rippled through the faithful gathered. This was followed by whispered titters and more giggles. Within minutes, the entire congregation knew what had transpired in our pew; only we were left confused and uncertain about the error that we had obviously committed.

Safe within the haven of our home once again, we dared to consult the dictionary in an attempt to understand our faux pas.

"What did I say again?", Gerard demanded to know, rifling through the tired pages of the book.

"You said 'shit.' I think you meant 'sit.' I wonder what 'shit' means. Why don't you look it up, try s-h-i-t." I spelled it phonetically in Dutch, slowly, carefully, uncertainly.

"It's not in here, and that's not a good sign," Gerard groaned, looking up at me from the page with eyes that showed hints of amusement and despair all at the same time. "I bet I've really done it this time! Come to think of it, I've heard the men around here use that expression, and I think it means . . .," he translated for me that lovely little word which we had just learned, and would never forget again.

"And to think I said that in CHURCH of all places! No wonder the people were so amused! Me in a suit, trying to be respectful, and then I open my mouth . . .", his voice trailing as he shook his head in self disgust.

"But they weren't laughing at us, just at our error. They weren't scornful, no, they smiled encouragingly in our direction after the service, didn't you see that? They were telling us not to give up, to keep trying," all this from me who hardly dared to open her mouth in a public place!

"And you have to admit it WAS funny," I added cautiously, glancing over to Gerard who smiled and nodded reluctantly.

Needless to say, our entrance into the church the following Sunday was considerably more subdued and timid. Neither of us attempted a word of English. The brief reprieve that we had earlier provided from the prevailing stern atmosphere of the House of God had not been forgotten however; the crowd still tittered goodnaturedly and smiled in our direction. I suspect it will be some time before this little blunder of ours is forgotten!

Lately I've taken to roaming through this vast expanse of a house, wandering from room to unused room and wondering about the people who lived here at one time. Some of the empty rooms are adorned with three or more varieties of yellowed, water-stained wallpaper and everywhere the ceiling plaster is decorated with an intricate maze of both tiny cracks and gaping fissures.

The large, musty attic, with its rough-hewn beams rising from either end of the house and coming together to form an obliging peak over its centre, is a summer haven for spiders, house flies, and probably a variety of other insects. In its dark, low recesses where the ceiling meets the attic floor are stored stacks upon stacks of magazines, school textbooks, and church hymnals. The entire attic is littered with abandoned religious statues and other church items, broken furniture, and piles of wood.

It seems that the Fathers gradually transposed this unused attic into a permanent resting place for religious items no longer needed but considered much too sacred to cart off to the local dump! Surely ours is the only attic for miles around to be graced by the serene, cherubic faces of the saints, and to house the complete and massive set of tabloids depicting the Stations of the Cross!

The attic is also littered with remnants of the farm's previous owners, the Brown family. The simple farm tools and the broken pieces of horse harness that line the west wall, the crude homemade child's sleigh and the odd tattered remnant of clothing, these items all serve to remind me that others have lived here before us.

According to the Fathers, three generations of Browns have lived on this farm. Ambrose Brown, the patriarch of the last generation, had a family of seven children, the youngest of whom is studying for the priesthood with the Salesians. All seven children were born in this house and I have difficulty envisioning how they survived the harsh winters. Mrs. Brown must have been a resourceful and optimistic woman to provide for such a large brood in these sparse surroundings.

For years the Browns struggled with the farm but failed to make it thrive. Finally, discouraged and approaching his senior years, Ambrose reluctantly sold the property to the Salesians.

At one time, this property also housed a fox farm; the evidence of this enterprise still exists in the west pasture: everywhere strands and bits of chicken wire rise up from the ground, an ever present menace to farm machinery and livestock alike. No amount of tugging will free the tenacious wire, the only way to eradicate the field of this hazard is with a pick and shovel. Needless to say, that unsavory task is painfully slow and backbreaking.

All this thought about what has transpired here before us makes me wonder what our place will be on this farm. Will we, with our youth, vigorous health, and determination manage to carve out a good life for ourselves here? Will the laughter of our children ring through these empty, waiting bedrooms in the years to come? Already the Fathers have indicated that they might sell this place. When that time comes, will we be able to, indeed will we desire to purchase it and make it truly our home? Or will we simply pack our belongings and move on one day, leaving only a few clues in the attic to add a short chapter to the history of this farm?

Only time, with its perpetual penchant for holding the secrets of the future, will tell.

19.

The Driver's License

We are a threesome once again; Antoon and Fie have ventured out on their own. Ironically, in their search for work for the winter, they have ended up on the Black farm, a place I would not return to in a million years! They will have their own little house, however, and that should be a vast improvement over the live-in situation we had to endure. Still, I do not envy them!

"Don't worry about us," Antoon said, dismissing our words of caution with a wave of his hand. "They wouldn't dare try anything with us! We'll be on our own and they will have absolutely no business with us beyond working hours."

On October 29, Antoon and Fie became the parents of a healthy baby boy. As I had done mere months before, Fie travelled alone by taxi to hospital. At home we held vigil with Antoon who anxiously awaited the news that a child of his had been born.

Mere days later Fie and her new baby, Hubert, returned to the farm, he bellowing at the top of his lungs as if to herald his own arrival. In the days that followed, little Hubert often entertained us with his lusty cries!

On these occasions Antoon, the ever-proud but inexperienced father, would eye his wife wearily and ask in a doubtful tone of voice, "Should he be crying this much?"

We will miss Antoon and Fie, especially the camaraderie that we enjoyed in the evenings when the day's work was done. We probably won't see them at least until next spring; the winter climate will make the roads impassable, and our wood-heated house would freeze up if we were to leave it for any amount of time.

Among the possessions that left with them was the refrigerator, that gleaming symbol of a modern, efficient kitchen! So once again I am carefully negotiating the steep flight of stairs to the dimly lit cellar on a daily basis. Besides storing our milk and other perishables there, the cellar also houses the bounty of the garden. A bin of potatoes sits in a dark corner and turnips and heads of cabbage line a nearby shelf. From the low ceiling hang bunches of onions and a rustling collection of brown beans waiting to be shelled. As well, suspended on makeshift meat hooks is the occasional piece of salted pork or back bacon which will keep for a short period of time.

I do enjoy the many smells of the cellar — the earthy scent of the potatoes that mingles with the more pungent odour of the turnips and the hint of saltiness that lingers in the cool air.

This year we are better prepared for the coming season in other ways. A recent highlight was a trip to town to buy some winter clothes. Although we could not afford an entire winter wardrobe, we did splurge on some long underwear, new work pants for Gerard, and ear muffs for each of us. Our mothers have also been busy knitting hats, scarves, mittens, sweaters and socks for the three of us, items we will cherish when the fury of winter is again unleashed.

Another betterment is the replacement of the old kitchen stove by the Fathers. I don't know much about stoves but apparently this one is designed to provide heat as well as a cooking surface and oven. According to the Fathers, the old stove was never meant to be a heat source and thus was woefully inefficient in that regard. In any event, I joyfully welcome the arrival of the new stove and regard it as a trusted companion to help us get through the winter!

114

We have recently made a major investment, one that will further our journey to independence and self-sufficiency. For two hundred and fifty precious dollars we have purchased a used truck, a 1948 half-ton Chevrolet. Gerard seems pleased with this acquisition; no longer will we have to rely so completely on the kindness of the Fathers for our transportation. However, we probably will not be using it much until the spring; our long lane will be so solidly blocked with snow throughout the winter.

Gerard has also obtained a driver's license, an experience that has proven to be totally different from anything he had expected. In Holland, driver education is mandatory and absolutely necessary to teach the student driver how to cope with the congested traffic. Here, the process of getting a license amounts only to "going for a drive" with someone from the local police department! Under his passenger's watchful guidance, Gerard negotiated the truck up and down the Jacquet River Hill and was then promptly presented with his license.

"Well, that was easy!", Gerard remarked upon his return. "In Holland that would have taken much longer and cost a lot more." It does seem as if owning a car here almost constitutes an automatic license to drive!

"I guess it's just another example of how easygoing the Canadians really are!", Gerard summed up the experience as he removed his coat and slipped it over the tarnished hook behind the kitchen door.

Gerard has decided that the truck will need a garage to protect it from the elements in the coming months. Hence, he has started to build one out of the "kist," the large wooden crate in which our possessions originally came to Canada. It seems like such an ungracious demise for the container that safely and uncomplainingly carried our entire store of worldly goods across the perilous Atlantic!

Not being one prone to sentimentality, the ever-practical Gerard has already knocked the crate apart and started to fashion a small shelter that will house only the front and hood of the truck. I imagine the finished product, in all its awkward incongruity, will do little to beautify the premises! Not that our yard, with its sporadic stacks of lumber and firewood and its haphazard cluster of gray, leaning outbuildings, could be considered even remotely attractive!

Jake Hensson is back in the neighbourhood, a sure sign that winter is on its way! Already he has come to "visit" a number of times. The Fathers have gently suggested that we not become too involved with the Henssons but poor Jake has been dealt a rather rough lot in life; to turn him away would be to sentence him back to that cold, cramped shack he calls home, and those strange, comfortless people that make up his family.

I predict that we will be seeing much of Jake in the coming months since he obviously enjoys Gerard's company and delights in my cooking! Gerard has already asked him to help cut and haul firewood throughout the winter. Although I have difficulty picturing Jake as being a great help, I am secretly pleased that Gerard will not be working in the woods by himself.

On this cold, dark November day I find my midriff slowly but unmistakenly beginning to expand once again. Although I don't relish the prospect of another long pregnancy, I joyfully welcome a second child into our little family, a child that will probably be born in April or May.

I pray that this pregnancy will be a bit easier; but already the incessant grinding and churning of my stomach have started to make things difficult. I vow to avoid hospitalization and fervently hope this child will not decide to come early.

Benny is doing so well now, he is a joy to behold. He is a contented baby with bright blue eyes and a sunny disposition. Often I will indulge in a study of his serene, sleeping face crowned with blond wisps of baby down, and think that, yes, we are truly blessed to be his parents. As best I know how, I will protect him from the extreme cold of winter, from the bitter, November east wind that is already whipping through the suffering treetops and sending the last of autumn briskly on its way.

20.

A Neighbour
Seeks Shelter

Winter, with all its magnificent fury and sparkling whiteness, has come to reside with us once again! It is as cold — no, even colder — than I can remember! I had almost forgotten what limbs that are blue and numb from the cold feel like, almost erased from memory the stinging, burning sensation of snow-filled boots against stockinged legs.

And yet, for all its hostility and seeming destituteness, the power of winter is a beauty to behold. Its calm silence on a clear, pristine day is complete and unending; its angry rage at the height of a ravaging storm is as deafening as the roar of a thundering freight train.

When the silvery mercury huddles in the very bottom of the outdoor thermometer, a similar drop in temperature occurs inside the house. Valiantly but in vain, the new stove tries to keep the kitchen warm. The same tired old pipes sometime glow to the point of dangerous, crimson translucence, a foreboding admonition to waste no time reducing the fire in the firebox.

We have been making full use of our winter wardrobe, wearing heavy sweaters and layers of woolen socks at all times. My tights and slacks are constant and uncomplaining companions!

Benny is a hearty little fellow who spends much of his day in the baby carriage near the stove. When his bedtime arrives in early evening he is bundled into his crib in our room, wearing mittens, a hat and many layers of clothing. He is snuggled under his covers with two hot water bottles, one at his side and one at his feet. Later in the evening, when the fire is allowed to die and the outdoor coldness quickly overwhelms the last struggling rays of heat in the kitchen, Gerard and I hasten into the cold bed, ungraciously attired in heavy socks and long underwear!

Maintaining a constant supply of clean diapers has proven to be a special challenge. Although the washing machine is a real boon, the soiled diapers have to be thoroughly prewashed by hand. They are then machine washed and rinsed by hand to ensure that no soapy residue remains. Finally, they are put through the machine wringer and arranged on a makeshift clothesline strung near the stove. The entire process is time consuming and tiring but at least our son has clean diapers to swaddle his tender little behind!

Our second Canadian Christmas was a quiet, family affair, highlighted with a wonderful parcel from Home. Again we decorated a small tree, exchanged little gifts and presented the baby with his very own store-bought rattle.

Because of the baby, we have been more housebound than ever and are taking turns going to church on Sundays. Our own truck is solidly buried under the snow so we still rely on rides to church with Christine's husband, Alex.

Our trek across the field to their house has become much easier, however, since Gerard discovered an old pair of snowshoes in one of the back sheds. Although they are awkward and anything but graceful, they are a vast improvement over sinking to one's waist with every tortured step. (I suspect that one should ideally be somewhat bow-legged in order to be proficient on these ungainly contraptions!)

One thing is certain: with these devices strapped to my feet I'm starting to feel more like a Canadian and less like an outsider. After all, is this not an outward sign that I too am becoming familiar with the Canadian ways of life?

Jake Hensson has moved in with us on a temporary basis. Neither Gerard nor I is exactly sure how this latest development has come about, all we know is that we felt sorry for this shivering, runny-nosed kid whose own family did not have room for him in their cold, crowded shack.

"You could stay with us for a few weeks," Gerard had casually suggested, at which Jake's dull eyes had lit up like one of the fancy neon signs in town.

Jake had insisted on sleeping near the stove, so an old overstuffed chair had been salvaged from one of the vacant rooms and placed in the kitchen. With a few blankets to cover him and a kitchen chair on which to prop his feet, he had settled happily into his new bed that first night.

"I keep the stove going," he had said, waving the poker as he snuggled deeper into the chair. We agreed, but warned him to keep the fire low.

Actually, it's been a real treat to wake up to a kitchen that is not stone cold and to have a fire already smoldering in the stove. As for Jake, it became apparent after his first night that he has a severe bed-wetting problem.

"Never mind," Gerard had said quietly to me. "That old chair is ready for the dump anyway. Couldn't we just set the cushion by the stove to dry?"

Needless to say, I have more washing these days but I really don't mind helping the poor soul. In his own little shack he would have surely frozen his wet loins by now!

Again I find myself anxiously counting the days until spring. With Gerard in the woods I find the days long, although I have many mundane tasks to keep me busy. Benny is a great comfort to me, the little one on the way is too. But oh . . . how I long for that distant sunny, summer's day when I will be proudly pushing the carriage containing my two precious little bundles. The delicious vision of that hot, leisurely stroll helps to keep the frigid arms of winter from enshrouding me completely, and prevents the looming snow drifts that peer at me through the fragile kitchen window panes from daring to advance any further.

21.

A Threatening Episode

We have had a most unsettling episode with the Henssons, one that has left me nervous and uncertain about being along during the day. No, it had nothing to do with Jake, that poor harmless fellow wouldn't hurt a fly.

Mere days ago, Jake had told us that his brother, Lawrence, had returned from Germany where he had been stationed with the Canadian armed forces. Late afternoon a day or so later, this Lawrence who had obviously had too much to drink appeared unsteadily on my doorstep to introduce himself "to the new neighbours." Somehow he made his way into the kitchen and demanded to see the baby. I became increasingly frightened as he swaggered roughly around the room, yelling and raising his fists abusively.

Fortunately Gerard was in the barn and came running when I stuck my head outside the porch door and called for him frantically.

Once inside the kitchen, Gerard eyed the stranger steadily and calmly and said, "You're drunk. Go home." The bully stood his ground, and cast a sullen, dark look our way. Quickly Gerard advanced toward him, grabbed him by the collar and threw him over his shoulder. Still calm, he commanded, "You are going home. Right now."

With the drunken, crumpled burden slung over his shoulder, Gerard started to trudge his way across the field to the Hensson shack. Halfway there, Lawrence suddenly half jumped, half slid off Gerard's back and fled staggeringly to his home.

"I don't think he'll be back," Gerard reassured me as I tried to console the screaming child who had been rudely awakened by all the commotion.

"If you had been in the woods, if you hadn't come when I called, I . . . I don't know what he would have done," my words came out in nervous, breathless puffs.

As we were still talking a gunshot reverberated loudly in the yard. I flinched instinctively and Gerard spoke tersely, his jaw hardening, "He's back. Take Benny and go into the cellar. I will call the Fathers."

As I hastened down the cellar steps, I could hear Gerard's low urgent voice on the telephone. A moment later he appeared at the top of the steps saying, "The Fathers are calling the police. They'll be here shortly. You stay down there."

"And what about you? Where are you going? He'll shoot you!", I pleaded with him to join us in the cellar.

"I'm just going into the porch to see if I can spot where he is. Don't worry, he's so drunk he couldn't hit a target if his life depended on it! I'll be careful."

From our dark haven, I could hear Gerard's footsteps as he made his way across the porch floor overhead. Silently he perched himself near the door and peered out cautiously.

"I see you there, you . . . !!", an angry, drunken voice screamed out suddenly, unleashing a string of abusive words at Gerard. This was followed by another gunshot, the sound of which stopped my heart in sheer terror.

Seconds later, Gerard reappeared at the top of the stairs. "The police are making their way up the lane. You stay down there! That fellow's gone crazy out there!"

Briskly the police arrested the drunken bully and charged him with trespassing. In vain they searched the snowbanks for a weapon.

"I think his father is around here too. A while ago I caught sight of him peering out from behind a fence post over there," Gerard pointed in an easterly direction. One of the officers slowly swept a searchlight across the darkening snow drifts in the direction Gerard had indicated.

"He's probably fled to his shack," the officer concluded when the light failed to reveal the hidden figure. "We'll take this one with us," he thumbed his hand at the cowering Lawrence. "He won't give you any more trouble."

After the police had left, Gerard laboured his way through the deep snow to the area where he had seen the senior Hensson. He found him there, hovering drunkenly in a hollow between two large drifts.

"Please don't send my son to jail," the elder Hensson slobbered. "He's only a boy, a wild kid. You know what young kids are like!"

"Go home!", Gerard commanded coldly and menacingly. "And if I ever catch you or him around here again . . .", his angry voice trailed as Hensson hurriedly picked himself up and retreated in the direction of his shack.

Back in the kitchen, we tried to reassure ourselves that this was just an isolated eposide, that something like this would never happen to us again. And yet, I will remain uneasy about it for a long time, knowing that armed bully resides a mere pasture's length from us.

Since leaving the Black farm, our security and safety are things I have spent little time worrying about. Now I find myself again wondering whatever possessed us to uproot ourselves in the first place, shun our comfortable environment, and set out for totally unknown territory.

Perhaps we are not the sensible, judicious couple we had thought ourselves to be. No, perhaps we are instead two reckless fools bent on tempting fate to its mysterious and perhaps horrifying limits.

22.

Gentle Prince

A beautiful daughter has been born to us, a wonderful new addition to our little family, a dear sister for Benny! We have given her the name, "Trudy," after my mother, Gertruida. She is a robust little thing with a beautifully pink complexion, a wisp of dark blonde hair, and those same clear blue eyes that Benny has.

She arrived on the 29th of April and mere days later we were both able to return home. After Benny's long ordeal, it was a luxury to walk out of the hospital with a healthy baby in my arms! She seems to have settled in without a hitch, and is apparently thriving on her routine. Indeed, her health is as vigorous as Benny's was frail!

These days I experience a lightheaded happiness as I tend to the needs of my two little ones and herald the arrival of spring. Already I have been hopelessly seduced by the first tantalizing signs of summer — the increasing strength of the sun, the tight green buds on every tree and bush, even the weeds and bull thistle that are springing up everywhere in their greedy haste to procure the choicest, sunniest spots in the yard.

Our truck, which sat partially nestled under the kist in a state of torpor throughout the winter, has been traded for a 1948 Chevrolet sedan. Now we can travel in the style of the modern Canadian family! I say 'modern' rather than 'average' since a car in this community is still a luxury, a commodity that many families are doing without.

In my exuberance over our new car, I must not forget our faithful horse, Prince, who has provided us with loyal service and dependable transportation over yet another long winter. Again and again he patiently applied his massive shoulders to the collar of his harness and plodded up and down the lane pulling the squeaky, cargo-laden bobsled behind him. Although I have never had a great love for horses, I must confess that this gentle giant has captured a tiny corner of my heart.

It seems that one of the Brown girls was a teacher who taught in a one-room school in Mitchell Settlement, a few miles from here. For years Prince was the horse that provided her with daily transportation to the tiny school, waiting patiently by its door for the school day to end and then delivering his mistress safely home again.

Now, in his advancing old age, he is still a graceful, handsome creature, good-natured and eager to oblige the wishes of his master.

A few days ago, early on a sunny afternoon, one of the neighbourhood odd-job men came to the door with handmade baskets to sell. Previously, I had only seen this gruff looking, burly, middle-aged fellow from a distance; now I eyed him cautiously as he stood shyly and uncertainly on my doorstep.

"Come in, Alphonse!", Gerard called from inside the kitchen. "What brings you to visit us today?"

The stocky, flannel-shirted figure hesitated at the door, glanced dubiously around the kitchen, and then advanced a few steps into the room. On one side he carried an assortment of woven baskets, their wooden handles looped around his arm. Under the other arm he carried a large laundry basket.

"I make baskets," he spoke in a low, gravelly voice. "To sell. I make them out of the alder bush. They're good baskets. Strong. Cheap. You want to buy one?" With that, he looked directly at Gerard as if he, rather than I, would be in the market for a basket!

"How much, Alphonse?", Gerard asked patiently. To me he quickly asked in Dutch, "What do you think?"

"I like the large one," I replied. "It would make a fine laundry basket and would also serve as a car bed for the baby."

"How much for the big one, Alphonse?", Gerard turned to our visitor.

Encouraged by this question, Alphonse replied enthusiastically, "Three dollars. Only three dollars. It is a good strong basket." He set it on the floor and motioned an invitation to me to examine it more closely.

"I'll give you two," Gerard declared.

Alphonse shook his head emphatically. "No. No, no. I need three." He held up three stubby fingers for emphasis. "It is a good strong basket," he repeated while Gerard pondered a decision.

"All right, Alphonse. Three dollars for the big one." Gerard extracted three tattered dollar bills from his wallet.

"Thank you," Alphonse spoke in a low, throaty voice and reached eagerly for the money. "You want to buy some more?", he added suddenly as if that possibility had just struck him.

"No, that's fine, that's it for now," we shook our heads simultaneously.

The peddlar proceeded to gather together the remainder of his collection which had been scattered on the floor, grunting heavily with the strain of bending over and reaching. Finally, with all the basket handles looped securely around his short, thick arms, he straightened up slowly, his face reddened from the sudden exertion.

Carefully he manouevered himself sideways through the doorway. I was about to close the door behind him when he abruptly stuck his head back into the kitchen.

"I give haircuts too!," he announced loudly to Gerard who was still sitting at the table with the last of his lunch on his plate.

"Okay, Alphonse. We'll remember that," Gerard replied noncommittally, waving at the retreating figure. "And thanks for coming today."

As I closed the door and resumed my place at the table,

Gerard cast me a mischievious glance and chuckled, "Maybe Alphonse can do your next haircut!"

In the past few weeks, our telephone has been ringing constantly, though rarely are the calls for us. Ours is what the Fathers call a "party" line, a term that aptly describes the way the telephone is often used in this community! Most of our calls are made to the Fathers; when Gerard lifts the receiver to place a call, there is invariably a lengthy, noisy, six-way conversation taking place. On a rare occasion when the line is free and our call is successfully placed, it is not long before the telltale clicks signifying that we have been joined by other curious ears, can be heard. Needless to say, our calls are kept brief and impersonal.

Jake Hensson no longer resides with us; he has returned home and will probably soon be embarking on his own mysterious adventures and summer ramblings. To our great relief, his bullying brother, Lawrence, seems to have left the area as well. Finally I am daring to breathe easier and to feel secure in my surroundings once again.

The Fathers continue to be wonderfully supportive of us and have become true and dear friends. We always look forward to their jovial visits and they seem to take genuine delight in us and in our children. We could not have been "stranded" near a better and more caring group of people. As long as I live I will be grateful to them for the unrestrained love and kindness they have shown to a young foreign family struggling to become truly Canadian.

23.

The Catalogue Order

I am finding it difficult to contain the joyous surge that seems intent on bursting my heart: WE ARE GOING TO HOLLAND FOR CHRISTMAS! Sometime during the summer we started to indulge in little fantasies about suddenly appearing on our parents' doorstep, our two little darlings in tow. Our whimsical fantasies turned to more serious contemplations as we began to examine the possibility of making this dream come true.

Financially, we knew that the dream was within reach. Although we have very little money here in Canada, we had left behind some savings in Holland, money that the Dutch government would not allow its countless emigrants to take with them. We knew that this money could be used to pay for our passage, provided the tickets were booked and paid for in Holland.

"Oh, let's!", we kept urging each other eagerly, as the idea began to take hold in our minds. "That money is really no good to us where it is. This way, we can go home and visit our dear ones and use up the rest of our money to buy some quality winter wear for the babies and ourselves."

"Yes, let's go!", we had finally decided, when one of us came up with a further suggestion, "Why don't we write to Gonda and Marinus and see if they want to come too!" Gonda and Marinus in California had meanwhile parented two children and I was equally eager to see them again and to meet their family.

"Excellent idea. You write to them," Gerard had said.

Mere days later Gonda's enthusiastic response had arrived in the mail. "A wonderful idea," she had written. "We've been having similar daydreams ourselves! Let's travel the ocean crossing together. We could take the train to Halifax and meet you there. Oh, what a wonderful idea!"

We have written to my parents of the news and asked them to make all of our travel arrangements. We plan to go in November and return sometime in January.

Another reason these plans are all being made possible is that Gerard's younger brother, Hugo, has come to live with us. In our absence, Hugo will look after the farm. A handsome lad of about twenty-one, he arrived in June with grand ideas about Canada and Canadian standards (translation: everything is enormous!). He harbors a youthful enthusiasm about seeking and finding his own fortune and seems intent on staying on this side of the Atlantic "forever."

Unhesitatingly he has begun to socialize with the neighbours who regard his fair complexion and near-white hair with something akin to awe. Already he has a following of young girls from the village who vie for the attention of this stranger who is physically so unlike them. And Hugo, of course, basks in the afterglow of all this attention.

When we once carefully suggested that he approach his new-found social life with just a bit more restraint, he responded flatly, "Yes, fine, but I'm not going to wait as long as you two did to get married!"

In any event, Hugo will be managing the farm while we are away, an arrangement that the Fathers have readily agreed to. However, in Gerard's own words, "that boy will need some training and discipline before we go."

There is much to do, especially now that we plan to be away from the farm for several weeks. The Fathers recently purchased a canning machine for us and I have been starting to can produce from the garden. What a luxury it will be to enjoy homegrown vegetables in the middle of winter!

I have also been making head cheese, using a recipe of Mrs. Olive's. Although the end product is tasty, the process is rather messy and tedious: the entire pig head has to be boiled for a long period of time, the meat then has to be painstakingly picked off the skull and ground, using a small hand grinder, and finally seasoning is added. Nevertheless, I am canning much of the head cheese and derive great satisfaction from lining the basement shelves with the gleaming cans of preserved food for the winter ahead.

We are once again in the middle of haying season and Hugo's strong back is of great help to Gerard. I thoroughly savor the heady perfume of the fresh cut grass that reaches my nostrils through the open kitchen window as yet another load of hay is trundled into the yard and forked into the hay loft. I will never, ever tire of the sights and sounds of summer, and now that we are going to Holland, winter truly seems a universe away!

Recently I was rather disappointingly initiated into the world of catalogue sales. Mrs. Olive had handed me a glossy catalogue on one of my outings to the post office, saying, "Now if you want something dear, you just pick it out and bring along your money and I'll send the order for you."

Like an excited child I had thumbed through the beckoning pages of the catalogue, my eyes lingering long and wistfully on the colorful selection that seemed limited only by my own meagre finances. Page after page of merchandise was temptingly presented, for the house, for the lady of the house, her husband, her children, even the family dog.

Finally, after much whimsical contemplation, my heart had settled on an inexpensive green print dress adorned with white pom pom ties. I pictured myself looking smart and fashionable in this new dress upon my arrival in Holland, surely causing my mother and sisters to remark:

"Sjaan looks so happy and well-rested!"

"And so smart in that stylish outfit!"

With Mrs. Olive's help, the order was soon on its way. Impatiently I awaited the arrival of the brown paper parcel that would contain my first new dress in over two years. When it finally arrived, I eagerly snipped away the string and tore at the paper as Gerard watched with a hint of amusement written on his face.

Triumphantly I held the dress up in front of me and stood waiting for Gerard's initial reaction. "Well, . . . hmm it seems a little big for you, and I'm not sure about the color, maybe you'd better just try it on."

Already my spirits were clouding as I slipped into the dress which I could see was much too large even before I had zipped it up. The material was flimsy and the big, brassy pom pom ties served to cheapen the dress even more. In front of the flecked old mirror I felt like an ungainly circus clown; my disappointment was intense.

"Why don't you just return it and order something else," Gerard suggested kindly, slipping his arm around my waist and glancing at me in the mirror. "This dress does nothing for you."

"But I don't even know if it can be returned," I complained loudly. "And even if I order something of a better quality, I still have no idea about sizes around here! Look at this dress! The size numbers in the catalogue tell me nothing! I suppose it would help if I could read the ordering directions!" By now I was feeling very sorry for myself.

"Christine will help you send it back," Gerard tried to console me. "Maybe we can go to town soon and pick out a dress for you."

Christine was eager to help me out of my dilemma. "Don't worry, Dear," she soothed as she poured over the instructions for returning merchandise. "Sometimes it isn't at all what it seems like in the catalogue. Do you want to order something else?"

I shook my head woefully, having resolved to curtail all shopping activity until my sisters and I set foot in the city of Leiden. I will just have to arrive at the Port of Rotterdam wearing one of my old but trusty outfits!

But Oh! I have absolutely nothing to complain about! After all, my wildest dreams are being realized! Any day now, my parents will be receiving our letter in the mail; how I daydream about the joyous upheaval our news will cause:

"Sjaan and Gerard are coming home!"

"Gonda and Marinus too, God bless us all!"

132

"And the children too, don't forget the children, all four of them!"

"It will be a wonderful, wonderful Christmas!"

Already I am counting the days to the moment of blissful reunion. Will they see any changes in us? Will we and our ways have become somewhat foreign, even "Canadian" to them? Will our Canadian children seem different from the other toddlers in the village? And what of Gonda with her American family?

Yes, we've changed, are changing constantly. But not enough to cease to savor the anticipation of a cup of real Dutch coffee, a pot of Mother's chicken and noodle soup, a family gathering around the kitchen table, a lively chat with friends at the local café! This Dutchness will never leave me, will never be erased from my character. And this, perhaps, is what I have been missing most of all: the close-knit Dutch camaraderie that can only be found in small, crowded, bustling communities, a camaraderie that will always remain elusive in an area such as this, so large and sparsely populated that neighbours may not see each other for months on end.

24.

The Binding of Ties, The Loosening of Ties

Another chilly, rainy Sunday afternoon has settled around us like a damp, woolen blanket. Outside the kitchen window the merciless wind is whipping the last of autumn out of the cringing, defenseless treetops. The babies are napping beneath layers of cozy quilts and Gerard has nestled into a comfortable armchair near the warm stove, armed with the latest edition of the "ILLUSTRATIE."

Hugo has gone off to visit the neighbours and I sit reading and rereading the latest letter from my parents. Everything has been confirmed, it is all coming true, we really are travelling to Holland next month!

We will travel by train to Halifax on November 22. There we will join Gonda and her family, and spend the night at The Hotel Nova Scotian which is supposedly in the vicinity of both the train station and the ocean terminals. The following day, November 23, we will board the Dutch liner, the s.s. *Maasdam*, and embark on an ocean voyage that will last approximately one week.

"Sjaan, you must think about something else for a while! Our trip is still a month away!", Gerard stirs in his chair and breaks the silence teasingly, trying to disguise his own eagerness to be reunited with his family.

Yes indeed! I must force my mind to be preoccupied with other things or else be faced with the prospect of having the next month inch by at a snail's pace.

I rise to check on my sleeping children who are recovering from severe colds. Today they are finally resting comfortably but just last week they were both struggling to breathe, their tiny phlegm-filled noses and throats labouring constantly to usher air inwards. Both were hot, flushed, and listless and neither was interested in food.

Gerard and I worried aloud but tried to reassure each other that this was only a bout of the common cold. Still I fretted about the possibility of pneumonia, that insidious sickness that had only recently threatened young Benny's very existence.

On one of the evenings that I was busy with the sick children, the staccato rap of a knock had suddenly sounded on the old kitchen door. There stood Mrs. Olive, our postmistress, her kind eyes full of concern.

"I just thought I'd come by and have a look at your babies," she explained as I took her coat. "Gerard looked so worried today when he came to pick up the mail. He told me they were quite sick."

Gratefully I led the way to where the little ones lay. Deftly, and with the experienced eye of a mother who has successfully raised a large brood of her own, she picked them up and looked them over, each in turn, clucking soothing little noises at them.

"They'll be just fine, Dear," she nodded after a moment or two. "They just have bad colds but should be starting to do better soon. Don't worry if they don't eat, just make sure they get lots to drink," she spoke reassuringly as she tucked the blankets around the little bundles.

"Do you think there's pneumonia?", I dared to ask, almost breathlessly.

"Oh, gracious, no, Dear, there's no reason to worry about pneumonia!", she shook her head vigorously as if to dispel an utterly foolish notion. "The worst of their colds is already over. They'll be better in a day or two." She took my hand and patted it reassuringly.

"Gerard told me you are going to Holland for Christmas," she suddenly changed the subject. "How wonderful! You must be very excited." I nodded wordlessly, my heart cartwheeling at having again been reminded of this delicious fact.

"Don't forget to come back . . . we'll miss you," she added softly, quietly, while struggling an arm into her heavy coat. She raised her head to smile at me, her gentle liquid-gray eyes staring momentarily into mine. Abruptly she looked down at her chest and busied herself with the large buttons on her coat.

Wordlessly she departed into the night, leaving me standing in the middle of the kitchen, engrossed in my own thoughts. Until now I had never even considered the possibility that our new neighbours might actually miss us and worry about our leaving here permanently.

All my thoughts and fantasies had centered on our arrival in Holland, the joyful reunion, the family celebrations, and yes, even the inevitable heartbreaking departure that would mark the end of our blissful hiatus.

Now, here, in another part of the world, a world that had been totally unknown to me a mere two years earlier, a gentle lady had quietly confessed that she would miss us and hoped that we would soon return to their community. Dear Lord, could it be true then, that we are actually becoming a part of this community, neighbours to help or be helped as needed, friends even, with those destined to share our daily, weekly, and seasonal course of living?

Yes, yes it must be true, I abruptly realized, sinking slowly onto a nearby kitchen chair. It must really be true, for here I am, suddenly missing them too. I will miss Dear Mrs. Olive, and the kind, softspoken Mrs. Delphis. Then there are Imelda and Christine, the raucous card players, and Margie and all the others too. And I will sorely miss the wonderfully kind Fathers, our true friends, guides and mentors.

That cold January day when we will again have to take leave of our Homeland and families is a day whose dawning I am already dreading. But coming Home to Canada, to our chosen country, and to the little community that welcomes our return, this is the part of our voyage that will make us realize that here is where we've elected to carve out a life for ourselves and our children. The bonds with our family will remain as strong as ever; the bonds with our former Homeland will be gently loosened to make way for new ties, to be formed gradually but steadily over the years to come.

25.

Endings and Beginnings

The clock is mere minutes away from midnight and yet sleep is elusive. I should be exhausted from packing, organizing, cleaning, and preparing for a two-month leave from my little domain; yet, here I sit, feeling more alive and animated than ever, an unquellable surge of energy spilling through my veins.

Early tomorrow morning Father Mario will drive us to the Jacquet River train station. Before leaving, Gerard will undoubtedly look in on his cows one last time. (No longer does he refer to them as mongrels, and indeed, they no longer resemble the lean, mangy beasts they once were!) Once more Gerard will pepper through his list of instructions to Hugo. Once more Hugo will listen intently, nodding his head rhythmically and occasionally interrupting Gerard's monologue with a plantive urge not to worry.

All is ready. Our little leather suitcases have been packed and filled to the breaking point and our train 'picnic' has been prepared. The children are sleeping peacefully, innocently unaware of the journey on which they are about to embark. This, after all, is the only home they have ever known. Gerard is slumbering soundly, not allowing his adrenalin to get in the way of a good night's rest.

And yet sleep continues to elude me as I rise soundlessly from my chair and begin to prowl quietly from room to room. This large, unpretentious, unadorned house, once strangely foreign and indifferent, now appears to beckon with comforting familiarity. Even the cracks in the plaster seem fixed into perpetual smiles of encouragement, and the shreds of wallpaper depicting opulent, gold-trimmed floral arrangements in elaborate baskets appear to herald a promise of the bounty to come.

Suddenly I become aware of an annoying sting in my eyes. Why, this is ridiculous, I admonish myself harshly. One does not become weepy over a house, certainly not this empty cavern of a house anyway. And yet . . . perhaps my sentiments are being spilled, not over the house that this is today, but rather, over the home that it will someday become.

Yes, yes, I realize with a sudden quickening in my pulse, already the transformation from house to home has begun in my heart. Even the yard, with its odd collection of landmarks has become a familiar friend. The pastures beyond, the little homes that dot the distant horizon, and the majestic hills that loom up from behind the clear blue bay to the north, have steadily but unsuspectingly been making their way into our hearts. This unassuming little corner of the world has become our niche.

On the eve of our departure, I am aware of how much I will miss all of this: OUR farm, OUR friends, OUR neighbours, OUR community, yes, our very future. I know now that we will return, for this is the destiny we have chosen and in which we have already invested so much of our efforts.

Quietly, peacefully, I slip into bed and lay my head upon the pillow. I sigh contentedly, knowing that tomorrow this little Canadian family will embark on a visit to dear and wonderful relatives, and to a former homeland.

Epilogue

In January of 1955, Gerard and Jane and their infant children returned to Canada and to the farm in northern New Brunswick. Shortly thereafter and true to the couple's predictions, the Salesian Fathers offered the property up for sale. With only a meagre savings account and few personal assets, Gerard and Jane saw no means possible to purchase the farm and worried further that they would be rendered homeless and jobless, and forced to start over once again.

They needn't have worried. Once more the benevolent Salesians chose to look out for the struggling young family. The farm's price tag had been set at $12,700 and included the house, barn, outbuildings, animals, machinery, and approximately 250 acres of land. The Salesians offered the farm to Gerard and Jane at this price, absolved the need for the usual down payment, and incredibly, suggested an arrangement whereby the entire cost of the farm could be gradually paid for in produce over the years to come.

Thus began the ritual of delivering milk to the Don Bosco College. Over the years, as the family grew, eager children went along for the ride. Their noisy antics were good-naturedly tolerated in the College kitchen and corridors. Indeed, the Salesians seemed to relish the presence of the fresh young faces and often indulged the children with a trinket, a marble or two, or a treat from the kitchen.

At the time of the sale, the Salesians went one step further by offering the young couple a $250 cash advance to purchase hay seed and seed oats. After all, they reasoned matter-of-factly to an overwhelmed Gerard and Jane, a young farmer just starting out needed quality seed if he was going to produce and harvest a plentiful crop.

On May 1, 1955, the ownership of the farm was officially transferred to the young Duivenvoordens. For the first time they were truly and permanently at home. With renewed fervor and high hopes, and no longer on salary, they strove to make a living on the modest farm. Firewood was offered for sale, and in 1957 they began selling milk on a contractual basis to the Crystal Dairy in Dalhousie Junction, some 40 kilometers away.

After a year on the farm, Hugo left to join his brother Antoon who had meanwhile found employment in a copper mine in Murdochville, Quebec. Several years later Hugo settled permanently in Windsor, Ontario, and Antoon (now better known as Anthony) and his family purchased a farm mere minutes away from Gerard and Jane. Gonda and Marinus also eventually came to Canada and settled in a nearby community.

The decade that followed was a difficult one for the Duivenvoordens, difficult both physically and financially. The days were long and exhausting for Gerard and Jane, and money was chronically scarce. A particularly trying January in the late 1950s left the family without electricity for ten days. That winter had been especially harsh and a January sleet storm had caused extensive damage to the community power lines.

For ten days, the couple struggled manually with the demands of a growing family and an ever-increasing number of farm animals. The greatest challenge involved maintaining an adequate supply of water for household and farm. Once more Prince and the ancient, creaking bobsled were pressed into service. The sled was outfitted with a number of old oil barrels which were filled by bucket with icy water from a nearby stream. Painstakingly and tediously, the animals were kept watered, and the dairy equipment and laundry were kept adequately clean.

Even so, it seemed that their valiant efforts to carry on as normally as possible were destined to be doomed by the sheer magnitude of the tasks at hand. With spirits dampening, they struggled to keep ahead of the thirsty demands of the dairy herd, and the ever-increasing collection of soiled diapers that sat patiently submerged in pails of acrid smelling water.

Looking back on this trying episode, Jane reminisces bemusedly that, "the power was suddenly restored on a late day in January, my birthday. It was the best birthday present anyone could have asked for!"

The 1950s saw many improvements made to the house, all in an attempt to more successfully ward off the bitter cold of winter. At a cost of one hundred dollars, a large, wood-burning furnace was acquired from a nearby church and installed in the basement. In exchange for a piece of property, a neighbouring handyman rebuilt the chimney and upgraded the basement walls with concrete blocks.

Although the new heating system was not an efficient one and hot water bottles continued to serve as a precious source of night time heat, Gerard and Jane recall that with the installation of the furnace and later an oil stove in the kitchen, "our really cold days were over."

In the years that followed, the family continued to increase in number: Catherine was born in 1955, Gerry in 1957, Nick in 1960, the twins, Pauline and Paul in 1961, and Carl in 1962.

By the late 1950s, Gerard and Jane were faced with the prospect of having to make a number of major business decisions, decisions that would profoundly effect their livelihood and future and that could no longer be postponed. In the preceding years the market for milk had become more lucrative and stable and the concept of farming for a living was gradually becoming viable. Nevertheless, a dairy operation had to be capable of producing a continuing and steady volume of milk if it was to compete successfully for a permanent share of the market and thrive on a long-term basis.

For Gerard and Jane, this meant the undertaking of a lifetime. In order to make their farm modern and competitive, the herd would have to be increased and the quality of the dairy animals upgraded. This also meant that the sagging, greying barn would no longer be adequate. As well, expensive dairy equipment would have to be installed, and inevitably, the collection of ancient farm machinery would have to be replaced.

The venture would require a bank loan of thousands of dollars and would call for a lifelong commitment to the farm. In the early 1960s, Gerard and Jane decided to take the plunge and in the summer of 1962 the construction of a large, modern dairy barn was begun.

During that busy year, Gerard and Jane quietly slipped away one morning to obtain their Canadian citizenship. In a brief ceremony that was conducted without pomp and fanfare, they were installed as Canadian citizens and officially welcomed to Canada. For Gerard and Jane it was a proud moment, a culmination of dreams realized, dreams that had at times seemed so elusive and remote.

The summer of 1962 was also a season filled with profound worry about the health of two of the children. Five-year-old Gerry and one-year-old Paul had both been diagnosed earlier as having aplastic anemia, a mysterious blood disorder about which little was known at the time. Both children had been hospitalized for considerable lengths of time; indeed, little Paul had spent so much time in the hospital that he remained a virtual stranger to his brothers and sisters.

Young Gerry, of feisty character but with eyesight rapidly failing, spent a happy summer hammering away at his own construction projects. Then, four days before Christmas, his resistance worn and his frail body ravaged with the disease, he suddenly succumbed to a severe bout of the flu. On route to the hospital, he died peacefully in Jane's arms.

For the grief-stricken parents, the loss of one of their precious children represented the greatest tragedy of all. Unlike any setback experienced before, this tragedy could not be overcome with optimism and hard work; rather, it marked a cruel finality that could only be helplessly grieved about.

As well, Gerry's death brought about the harsh realization that little hope remained for Paul. Even as the family sorrowed over the death of Gerry, they were faced with the struggle of somehow trying to prepare themselves mentally for the inevitable loss of another child.

Four weeks later, on January 17, 1963, the end came. Numbed and in shock, the family prepared for the burial of another of its beloved. Meanwhile, the cold wet winter dragged on, seemingly to signify the bleakest of times that had befallen Gerard and Jane.

The 1960s saw vast improvements made to the farm, home, and property. More land and better machinery were purchased. A Holstein pedigreed herd came to gradually replace the mixed collection of the previous decade.

Two more children were born to the family during those years: Jane in 1965, and Yvonne in 1967. Their arrival brought much joy to a family that, first and foremost, regarded their children as the most precious commodity of all. Indeed, a sense of happiness and well-being had settled over the household once again.

In 1971, Gerard and Jane proudly attended their first of many high school graduation ceremonies. Young Ben, an honours graduate, had already decided to follow in his father's footsteps and thus set about acquiring further education in agriculture. He returned home in 1973, college diploma in hand and ready to work on the farm that would, in all probability, one day be his.

With him he brought new plans and ideas, the implementation of which would see the further modernization of the farm. Over the years, two large storage silos were built and a major addition was made to the dairy barn. The farm, one of the few of its size in northern New Brunswick, was beginning to receive recognition as an efficient, well-managed enterprise.

Then, on October 30, 1976, the most disastrous and sorrowful of tragedies struck. Late on that day a tractor accident swiftly and inexorably claimed the life of 23-year old Ben. For Gerard and Jane it was a time of utter devastation, a time that saw the crumbling of goals that had been diligently pursued over a period of two decades. But mostly, it was a time of profound and uncontrollable grief that seemed to cast a permanent shadow over the heart and threatened to keep rays of happiness from ever shining there again.

As Gerard and Jane huddled together and remembered an earlier time when they had prayed for the survival of this child, their precious first-born lay immaculate and lifeless, a young life unfeelingly snuffed out by the very mechanization that he had earlier introduced to the farm.

The community, which by now had long considered the family as one of their own, gathered around the grief-stricken Duivenvoordens and offered their unfailing support. Food was offered in abundance and the children were looked after by close friends who stayed with the family and assumed charge during the days immediately following Ben's death.

Though few in the community were farmers by trade, many came to offer their help with the day-to-day operation of the farm. Much later, when the initial shock had begun to wear off, Gerard and Jane were able to remember that the community support had been tremendous.

"We were overwhelmed by the support and efforts of the community. There were so many who came and quietly did what they could for us. They could not undo our tragedy, nor could they take away our grief, but they did everything else for us. For that we'll always be grateful."

For a period of time following Ben's death, the future of the farm remained uncertain. Disheartened and seemingly depleted of all energy, Gerard and Jane talked of selling their property and moving their family elsewhere. But where would they go? What would they do? This farm had been their whole life and although it had dealt them the cruelest of blows, it seemed somehow that this was still truly where they belonged. In time the family made the unanimous decision to stay.

The decade that followed was a time for healing and growing, a time during which peace of mind and happiness were gradually restored. In due course the couple proudly saw each of their children complete high school, and many go on to college and university. They also celebrated the marriages of two daughters and contentedly saw each offspring in turn leave to pursue his own chosen goals.

Over the years some Dutch traditions have been actively maintained and enjoyed. The children remain fluent in the Dutch language, a boon to the many visitors from Holland who have graced the Duivenvoorden's bountious kitchen table. However, although rich in heritage and fortunate to be part of a larger, international clan, the family considers itself to be proudly Canadian.

Today Gerard and Jane are still actively involved in the management and operation of the farm. They are content knowing that their son, Nick, who has managed the dairy herd for several years, will assume ownership upon their retirement.

The family remains a close-knit one, and although

reunions are not frequent, they are joyous and festive occasions. As the conversation and eager chatter is bantered back and forth between siblings eager to catch up on each other's news, Gerard and Jane bask in the knowledge that a solid and happy family has been successfully raised.

On the eve of their thirty-sixth wedding anniversary, the couple looks back at an earlier time, a time when they were two uncertain immigrants alone in a foreign land.

"We've come a long way," they concede without hesitation, "and this is where we belong now. It just wouldn't feel right to us to be anywhere else. Because of the families we left behind so many years ago, Holland will always be a wonderful place to visit. But now 'Home' is here. And here is where we are truly and contentedly at home."